KNITTING FOR BEGINNERS

The A-Z Guide to Have You Knitting in 3 Days

By Emma Brown

"I like making a piece of string into something I can wear"

TABLE OF CONTENTS

INTRODUCTION

Knitting is the process which **produces cloth from thread**. It's used to create garments, toys, home wares and all sorts of exciting things! It's a skill that can be enjoyed by anyone – and it's growing in popularity every single day with celebrities such as Sarah Jessica Parker and Cameron Diaz happily declaring their love for the hobby. But, it's actually so much more than that. Knitting can be **beneficial to your health**! It has been proven to lower blood pressure, relax the enthusiast and even burn calories (*approximately 55 for half an hour of knitting*).

In fact, knitting has become so popular that there are now many competitions and challenges associated with it. The most well-known of these being:

The World's Fastest Knitter – currently held by Miriam Tegels of the Netherlands who can hand knit 118 stitches in one minute.

Speed Knitting – currently held by Linda Benne of America who can knit 253 stitches in 3 minutes.

The World Knitting Record – currently held by Australia at 4 hours and 50 minutes.

Of course, these aren't things that we are aiming for just yet! They are just interesting facts which demonstrate how widespread knitting has become. Although these days it is considered a hobby more popular with females, knitting started out as a male only occupation, proving that anyone can reap the benefits from it!

There are many suggestions of when knitting began, but the truth of it is no one *really* knows since many ancient textile fragments thought to be knitting have actually turned out to be an ancient form of needle craft, often thought of single needle knitting – *nålebinding*. However, when the knitting machine was invented, hand knitting became less of an essential necessity, and more of a hobby, which is where we are at today.

'*Knitting for Beginners*' is an **extensive guide to the basics of knitting** – giving you step-by-step instructions helping you to master all of the stitches and techniques that you'll need to get started with this brand new skill. Once you have gotten to grips with some of these, a few patterns have been included which will get you putting everything together in fun and interesting ways. Once you have completed these – anything else will become much easier in comparison.

In fact, this is the most comprehensive knitting guide for beginners available on the market, and once you have worked through everything within its pages, you'll never look back!

SUPPLIES

There are a few supplies that you will need before you start your first knitting project. The amount you spend on this skill is entirely up to you, and entirely depends on your requirements and budget. Everything that you'll need to complete a knitting pattern will be listed within the patterns information, but just **for practicing the stitches** listed in this guide, **you will only need the basics**:

- Yarn

- Needles

- Scissors

- A sewing needle

- A crochet hook.

Yarns

Yarn is a long continuous length of interlocking fibers. It's **essential to knitting as it is the basis for creating the cloth.** It may interest you to know that although we automatically think of wool at the mention of yarn, but for the four of five hundred years of the recorded history of knitting, the yarn materials were cotton or silk.

To decide **what yarn is best suited to a particular knitting project,** many factors come into play; its *loft* (its ability to trap air), its *resilience* (elasticity under tension), its *washability*, its *feel* (its feel, particularly softness vs. scratchiness), its *durability against abrasion*, its *tendency to twist or untwist*, its *overall weight and drape*, its *blocking and felting qualities*, its *comfort* (breathability, moisture absorption, wicking properties) and of course its *look*. Of course other factors may be considered, but don't worry – that isn't for you to worry about – the knitting pattern will tell you all the necessary information about which yarn is best suited for each individual project, but to understand the things a little better, you will want to know the details of everything discussed in this chapter.

There are three main **types of yarn:** wool, cotton and acrylic. Each type produces an entirely different result after it has been worked with, so it is important to familiarize yourself with these during the practice stages of learning this skill so you know how each one works and how they suit you and your knitting style.

When choosing a yarn type for your knitting project, consider the following:

- **Wool:** Wool (made from the fleece of sheep) is the queen of yarns, and it remains a popular choice for knitters. Here are some of your wool yarn options:

  - **Lamb's wool:** Comes from a young lamb's first shearing.

  - **Merino wool:** Considered the finest of the fine breeds.

  - **Pure new wool/virgin wool:** Wool that's made directly from animal fleece and not recycled from existing wool garments.

  - **Shetland wool:** Made from the small and hardy native sheep of Scotland's Shetland Islands.

  - **Icelandic wool:** A rustic, soft yarn.

  - **Washable wool:** Treated chemically or electronically to destroy the outer fuzzy layer of fibers.

- **Fleece:** Examples include mohair and cashmere, which come from Angora and Kashmir goats, respectively. Angora comes from the hair of Angora rabbits.

- **Silk, cotton, linen, and rayon:** The slippery, smooth, and often shiny yarns.

- **Synthetic:** Including nylon, acrylic, and polyester. Straddling the border between natural and synthetic are soy, bamboo, corn, and other unusual yarns made by using plant-based materials.

- **Novelty:** Novelty yarns are easy to recognize because their appearance is so different from traditional yarns:

  - **Ribbon:** A knitted ribbon in rayon or a rayon blend.

  - **Bouclé:** This highly bumpy, textured yarn is composed of loops.

  - **Chenille:** Although tricky to knit with, this yarn has an attractive appearance and velvety texture.

  - **Thick-thin:** Alternates between very thick and thin sections, which lends a bumpy look to knitted fabric.

- *Railroad ribbon:* Has tiny "tracks" of fiber strung between two parallel strands of thread.

- *Faux fur:* Fluffy fiber strands on a strong base thread of nylon resemble faux fur when knitted.

• *Specialty:* These traditional types of yarn create special looks in knitted items:

- *Tweed:* Has a background color flecked with bits of fiber in different colors.

- *Heather:* Blended from a number of different-colored or dyed fleeces, and then spun.

- *Marled (ragg):* A plied yarn in which the plies are different colors.

- *Variegated:* Dyed in several different colors or shades of a single color.

Yarn is **also categorized by weight**, which is shown on the label. The *Craft Council of America* has yarn organized into the following numbered categories:

1 or Super Fine   *(sock, baby and fingering yarn)*

2 or Fine   *(baby and sport yarn)*

3 or Light   *(light worsted and DK yarn)*

4 or Medium   *(worsted, afghan and Aran yarn)*

5 or Bulky   *(chunky, craft and rug yarn)*

6 or Super Bulky   *(roving and bulky yarn)*

These numbers are used by knitters and crocheters, and the table below explains exactly what these numbers mean and what needles and crochet hooks work best with them. Using the recommended needles with the yarn required will produce the best results.

Yarn Weight:	0 Lace	1 Super	2 Fine	3 Light	4 Medium	5 Bulk	6 Super
Types of Yarn in Category.	Thread, Cobweb, Lace	Sock, Baby.	Sport, Baby	DK, Light, Worsted.	Worsted, Afghan.	Chunky, Craft, Rug.	Bulky, Roving.
Knit Gauge Range in Stockinet Stich to 4 inches.	30 – 40 sts	27 – 32 sts	23 – 26 sts	21 – 24 sts	16 – 20 sts	12 – 15 sts	6 – 11 sts
Recommended Needle in Metric Size Range.	1.5 – 2.25mm	2.25 – 3.25mm	3.25 – 3.75mm	3.75 – 4.5mm	4.5 – 5.5mm	5.5 – 8mm	8mm and larger
Recommended Needle in US Size Range.	000 – 1	1 – 3	3 – 5	5 – 7	7 – 9	9 – 11	11 and more
Crochet Gauge Range in Single Crochet to 4 inch.	32 – 42 double crochets	21 – 32 sts	16 – 20 sts	12 – 17 sts	11 – 14 sts	8 – 11 sts	5 – 9 Sts
Recommended Hook in Metric Size Range.	Steel 1.6 – 1.4mm	2.25 – 3.5mm	3.5 – 4.5mm	4.5 – 5.5mm	5.5 – 6.5mm	6.5 – 9mm	9mm and larger
Recommended Hook in US Size Range.	Steel 6, 7, 8 Regular Hook b-1	B-1 to E-9	E-4 to 7	7 to I-9	I-9 to K10½	K10½ to M-13	M13 and larger

You will notice in the table above, something called a '***gauge***' is mentioned. This refers to the number of stitches per inch. It's measured by counting the number of stitches over several inches, then dividing this by the number of inches in the width of the sample.

It is recommended to **make a gauge swatch before starting a knitting project,** and details on how to do this will be included in the pattern. (A step-by-step guide for creating a gauge swatch will be in a later chapter of this book.) This will ensure that the finished piece will be the size you want it to be, that the yarn and needle size you've selected are suitable, and it will make sure all the stitches you create are even.

It is important to know **how to care for the yarn** you are using, so that the knitted projects you create from it are looked after effectively. The *universal symbols* you need to be aware of *are listed below:*

Care Instruction Symbols

Machine Wash Instructions	Special Care	Bleaching Instructions	Dryer Instructions		Ironing Instructions	Dry Cleaning
Normal Wash	Hand Wash	Bleach as Needed	Normal Dry	DO NOT Machine Dry	Low Heat	Dry Clean
Permanent Press	DO NOT Wring	Non-chlorine Bleach as Needed	Permanent Press	Line Dry	Med. Heat	Dry Clean w/ Any Solvent
Gentle Cycle		DO NOT Bleach	Drip Dry		High Heat	Dry Clean w/Petroleum Solvent
DO NOT Machine Wash			Gentle Setting	Dry Flat	DO NOT Steam	Dry Clean w/Solvents Other Than Trichloroethylene
Cold (<85°F) (<29.5°C)			DO NOT Tumble Dry	Dry in Shade	DO NOT Iron	DO NOT Dry Clean
Warm (<105°F) (<40.5°C)			No Heat			
Hot (<120°F) (<49°C)			Low Heat			
Hot (<140°F) (<60°C)			Normal/ Med. Heat			
Machine wash cold on gentle cycle			High Heat			

So as you can see from all the information provided in this chapter about yarn, it is **very important to take due care** when selecting the right texture, weight and fiber of the yarn for your knitting project to make sure the finished product is exactly what you want it to be. It is also absolutely vital to read the yarns label as that contains every bit of information you will need to know about the material. By **referring back to the weight chart, you can ensure you pick the right size needles to work with and you can also check up on the yarns gauge – or stitches per inch.**

Needles

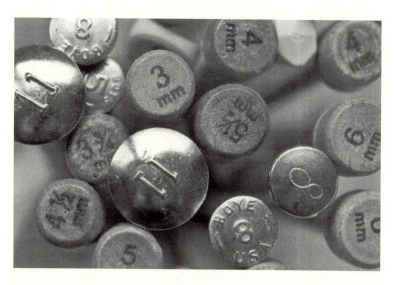

Selecting **the right knitting needles for your project is essential**. Choosing the wrong size for the yarn and pattern will throw off the gauge entirely and the end result will not look anything like you want it to. These needles generally have a long shaft and taper at the end and they come in a wide range of materials, including bamboo, aluminum, steel, wood, plastic, glass and casein. It may surprise you to learn that originally knitting needles were created from ivory, tortoise shell, or even bone! Although the *knitting needle size will be included in the pattern, the material* you select *is completely dependent on your personal preference*.

As stated before, needle size is very important to a knitting project. Patterns will often tell you the most suitable needle size, but it's always handy to be aware of the conversion chart:

Metric Sizes, mm	UK Sizes	US Sizes
2.0	14	0
2.25	13	1
2.75	12	2
3.0	11	-

3.25	10	3
3.5	-	4
3.75	9	5
4.0	8	6
4.5	7	7
5.0	6	8
5.5	5	9
6.0	4	10
6.5	3	$10^{1/2}$
7.0	2	-
7.5	1	-
8.0	0	11
9.0	00	13
10.0	000	15
12.0	-	17
16.0	-	19
19.0	-	35
25.0	-	50

As well as size, you need to pick the right type of needle for the knitting project. There are **three main types** that you will work with at some point.

Circular Needles – which contain a thin cable which joins two short needles. These are used for knitting in the round and can create anything from a neckband to a sweater.

Double-Pointed Needles – which have two pointed ends. They are perfect for making small tubes for cuffs and mittens, etc.

Straight Needles – which contain one blunt and one pointed end and they're generally used for flat knitting. The larger your project, the longer needle you'll need.

Experienced knitters will tell you that **it is much easier to start with straight needles** – especially when practicing stitches. Back and forth rows are constructed using the straight needles, whereas the circular and double pointed needles can be used to create rounds. It's much simpler to get to grips with rows as you know where they begin and where they end, whereas it takes a little more experience when it comes to rounds – as their name suggests they are circular.

The techniques for knitting in rows and rounds is discussed in more detail in a later chapter in this book, so if you want to be able to practice them all successfully, it might be a good idea to get hold of some of each type of needle before you begin. Use the size guide in the table above to help you where possible. It is always useful to have this handy because you never know when you might need it!

Holding Needles And Yarn

The next thing you need to know is **how to hold your selected knitting needles and yarn correctly**. Eventually you'll adapt and develop your own way of doing things, but it's always great to have a place to start. Here is a great step-by-step guide to this:

You hold the right hand needle as if it were a pencil. When starting your knitting and working the first few rows, pass the knitted piece over the right hand between the thumb and index finger. As the work progresses, let your thumb slide under the knitted piece, grasping the needle from below – as shown here.

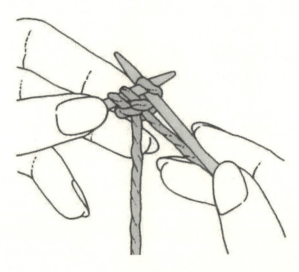

Hold the left hand needle over its top, using the thumb and index finger to control the tip of the needle.

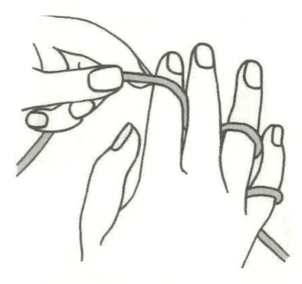

You hold the yarn in your right hand, passing it under your little finger, then around the same finger, over the third finger, under the centre finger and over the index finger. Use your index finger to pass the yarn round the needle tip. The yarn circled around the little finger controls the yarns tension.

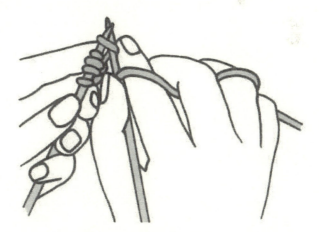

Alternatively, you can hold the yarn in your right hand and pass it under the little finger, over the third finger, under the centre finger and over the index finger. Use your index finger to pass the yarn to the needle tip. The tension is controlled by gripping the yarn in the crook of the little finger.

If you are left-handed, all you need to do is turn this around, so that the needle in you left hand is the one to do the majority of the work. There are more tips for left-handed knitters later on in this book.

Other Knitting Tools

The needles and yarn are obviously essential to starting a knitting project, but there are a few other items you should consider getting as they will make the hobby that much more easy and enjoyable:

Stitch Markers - Stitch markers **have many uses,** including: to mark a certain number of stitches, the beginning of a round, where to make a particular stitch, etc. Patterns may recommend using a stitch marker to help making the garment or product a much easier process.

Row Counters - A row counter is a tool which **allows you to record the amount of rows or rounds you have completed** so that you don't lose your place in a knitting pattern – particularly if a row is repeated a number of times. This allows you to leave your project and come back to it as required without ever forgetting how much you have left to do.

Needle Point Protectors - Knitting needle point protectors protect your knitting needles from damage, which means that they'll last much longer.

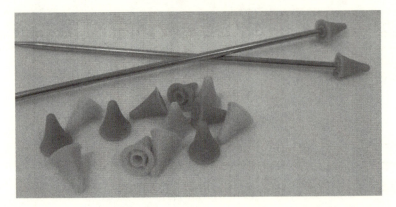

Stitch Holders - Stitch holders are used to hold open knitted stitches when not being used by the needles. This can be used when finishing off a side of an item, or to help shape an item.

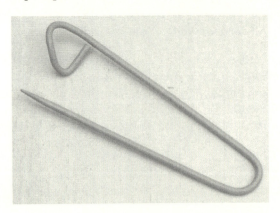

Crochet Hook - A crochet hook will often be used for embellishments in knitting, but sometimes people like to combine the two crafts.

UNDERSTANDING PATTERNS

The first **thing you need to know** about knitting patterns is the information they contain. They will always contain the following details:

Skill level – this is generally one of the very first things you'll see after the pattern name and picture. This information is useful to know as it will allow you to see if it's achievable. Sometimes this will be recorded as numbers 1 – 4 with one being the easiest.

Size – this is especially important for garments.

Gauge – this gives you the number of stitches per inch. The more you knit, the more this information will become vital to you.

Pattern information – this section will give you the details of everything you need to complete the pattern. It'll let you know what yarn, needles and other equipment you need. Although you don't have to follow this exactly, it's best to stick closely to the sizes suggested so that the pattern will turn out as you want it.

Pattern abbreviations – at a first glance, knitting patterns can seem very complex as they're written in abbreviations – and when you don't know what these mean, they can seem like a strange language. Below is a table of all of the standard abbreviations you are likely to come across.

Knitting Glossary Terms

The following are the **commonly used abbreviations**:

* *: Repeat the instructions between the two asterisks

[ ]: work instructions in brackets as many times as directed

( ): work instructions in parenthesis as directed (also used to indicate size changes)

Alt: It means alternate (Like the "alt rows")

Beg: It means begin/beginning

Bet: It means between

BO: It means bind off

CA: It means color A (This is the case where there is above one color is being used)

CB: It means color B (Just as above)

CC: It means contrasting color

Cm: Centimeters

Cn: It means cable needle

CO: Cast On

Cont.: It means continue

Dec: It means decrease

DK: It means double knitting (a yarn weight or knitting technique)

Dp, dpn: It means double/pointed needle

EON: It means end of needle

EOR: It means end of row

FL: It means front loop

Foll: It means follow or following

G: It means Gram

G st: It means garter stitch (knitting every row)

Inc: It means increase

Incl: It means including

K: It means knit

K1 f&b: It means knit into the front of the stitch and later on to the back of the similar stitch

K tbl: It means knitting through the back loop, which establishes a twist on the completed stitch

K2 tog tbl: It means knit two stitches together

K2tog: It means knit two stitches together through the back loop instead of the front

Kwise: Knitwise

LC: It means left cross, a cable stitch where the front of the cross slants to the left

LH: It means left hand

Lp: It means loop

LT: It means left twist, a stitch that creates a mock cable slanted to the left

M: Meters

M1: It means make 1 stitch, which requires an increase method

M1 p-st: Make one purl stitch

MC: It means main color

Mm: Millimeters

Oz: Ounce

P: It means purl

P tbl: It means purl through the back loop instead of the front

P up: It means pick up

P2tog: It means purl two stitches together

P2tog tbl: It means purl two stitches together through the back loop instead of the front

Patt: It means pattern

Pm: It means place stitch marker

Prev: It means previous

Psso: It means mean pass slipped stitch over (as in binding off)

Pu: It means pick up (stitches)

Pwise: It means purlwise

RC: It means right cross, a cable stitch where the front of the cross slants to the right

Rem: It means remaining

Rep: It means repeat

Rev St st: It means reverse Stockinette stitch

RH: It means right hand

Rnd: It means round(s); when knitting on a circular or double pointed needle when it means the yarn is joined, you knit in rounds, not rows

RS: It means right side

RT: It means right twist, a stitch that creates a mock cable slanted to the right

Sk: It means skip

Sk2p: It means slip 1 stitch, knit 2 together, and then pass the slipped stitch over the knitted ones to create a double decrease

Skp: It means slip 1 stitch, knit 1 stitch, and then pass the slipped stitch over the knitted one to create a single decrease

Sl, slst, slip: It means slip or slide a stitch without working it

Sl, k1, psso: It means same as "skp"

Sl1k: It means slip 1 stitch knit-wise

Sl1p: It means slip 1 stitch purl-wise

sl st: It means slip stitch

Ssk: It means slip 1 stitch, slip the next stitch, and then knit the 2 stitches together to create a left/slanting decrease

Ssp: It means slip 1 stitch, slip the next stitch, and then purl the 2 stitches together to create a right/slanting decrease

Sssk: It means slip 1 stitch, slip the next stitch, slip the 3rd and then knit the 3 stitches together to create a double, left/slanting decrease

St: It means stitch

Sts: It means stitches

St st: It means Stockinette stitch; alternately knit a row and purl a row

Tbl: It means through the back loop (of a stitch)

Tog: It means together

WS: It means wrong side

Wyib: It means with yarn in back

Wyif: It means with yarn in front

Yds: Yards

Yfwd: It means yarn forward (same as yarn over)

Yo: It means yarn over, move yarn to the opposite direction

Yrn: It means yarn 'round' needle (same as yarn over)

yon: It means yarn over needle

Knitting patterns also have **specific terminology, and this can vary from UK to US patterns,** so it is best to be aware of these so there is no confusion:

UK	US
Tension	Gauge
Cast on	Bind on
Cast off	Bind off
Stocking stitch	Stockinette stitch
Moss stitch	Seed stitch

So now that you've seen all the abbreviations and terminology, it is time to look at an example line from a pattern.

Row 1: *K2, P2; rep from * across, end K2.

Which means you will knit the first two stitches, then purl the next two stitches; then knit 2, and purl 2, again, and repeat the steps following the asterisk all across the row until the last two stitches which you will knit. If you break the row down in this way, you'll find it very easy to get to grips with a knitting pattern.

A knitting pattern **may ask you to knit in rows or rounds**. Of course, this will **determine which needles you use**. Straight needles are suited to back and forth rows, and circular and double pointed needles are best for knitting rounds. Later on, in the <u>Stitches</u> chapter, how to knit in these styles is shown with step-by-step directions. Here is an example of written knitting pattern:

KNITTED *Baby Bunting*

This Baby Bunting can be made with the following:
"DAWN" KNITTING WORSTED or
"DAWN" NYLON OF KNITTING WORSTED SIZE
19 ozs. Lt. Blue or Baby Blue or color desired.
1 pr. knitting needles No. 6.
Plastic crochet hook No. 6.
5 yds. blanket binding.
20-inch zipper.
GAUGE: 6 sts = 1 inch.
BUNTING: Cast on 166 sts and work in pattern as follows:
1st Row. * Y O, slip 1 st as to P, K 1, repeat from * across row.
2nd Row. * Y O, slip 1 st as to P, K the Y O and next st tog, repeat from * across row. Repeat 2nd row for pattern. Work even in pattern until work measures 26 inches from beginning, bind off (always working the Y O and next st together).
GUSSET: Cast on 8 sts, work in pattern increasing 1 st on each side every 3rd row 6 times (20 sts). Work even until gusset measures 14 inches from beginning. Then decrease 1 st on each side every 3rd row until 8 sts remain, bind off. With

"STAR" MERCERIZED SEWING THREAD, sew binding across 2 short sides and 1 long side. Fold so opening is at center, then sew gusset in position. Sew zipper in position.

HOOD
Starting at front of hood, cast on 68 sts and work in pattern same as on bunting for 6 inches.
Next 6 Rows. Bind off 7 sts at beginning of each row. Bind off remaining sts. Sew back of hood together. With right side toward you, pick up and K 58 sts across lower edge of hood. P 1 row.
Next Row. BEADING: K 2, * Y O, K 2 tog, repeat from * to within last 2 sts, Y O, K 2, P 1 row.
Next Row. K across and increase 12 sts evenly spaced. Then work in pattern for 3 inches, bind off.
TIE: Crochet a ch about 30 inches long and lace through beading. Finish with pompons.
POMPONS: Wind yarn over a 2 inch cardboard 32 times. Tie through center and cut both ends. Trim into shape and attach to each end of ties. Sew binding around front edge.

This is written in rows, and gives you an example of how you will work. In the Patterns chapter of this book, you will be given a few knitting patterns to practice ranging from beginner to advanced. Some of them will be written in step-by-step directions, the more advanced ones will be written as a traditional pattern is, with the rows described as above that you will have to separate into instructions. This will prepare you for when you move on from this book, and start knitting on your own.

Knitting Charts

Knitting charts are **graphic representations of knitting patterns**. They also illustrate exactly how the item will look once it has been knit, giving the user the advantage of being able to identify any mistakes quickly.

In a knitting chart, each square represents a stitch, similar to the way that each abbreviation in text instructions does. Before starting working from a knitting chart, you should **familiarize yourself with the meanings of the symbols used**.

Below is an example:

key and abbreviations

☐ **k** - knit

⊙ **yo** - yarn over

☑ **k2tog** - knit 2 together

◩ **ssk** - slip, slip, knit - slip 1 knitwise, slip 1 knitwise, put 2 slipped sts back on LH needle and k2tog through back loops

◼ **sl1-k2tog-psso** - slip 1 knitwise together, knit 2 together, pass slipped st over

chart: gothic lace
Repeat rows 1-12

edge sts   8 stitch repeat   edge sts

(worked 5 times per row for cowl, 4 times per row for scarf)

These charts can either show all of the rows, or sometimes they one show the 'right side' of the work. If the latter is the case, text instructions will also be included for how to work the **'wrong side' rows**.

all rows

chart: gothic lace
All rows shown

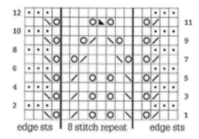

edge sts | 8 stitch repeat | edge sts

RS rows only

chart: gothic lace
Right-side rows shown, Wrong-side rows omitted.

All WS (even numbered) rows:
k3, purl to last 3 sts, k3

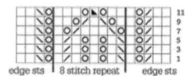

edge sts | 8 stitch repeat | edge sts

If the chart is '**right side**', you will typically work the stitches one at a time from right to left. The instructions for the 'wrong side' will be written next to the chart, as shown below:

RS rows only ::: read from right to left and from bottom to top of chart

chart: gothic lace
Right-side rows shown, Wrong-side rows omitted.
All WS (even numbered) rows:
k3, purl to last 3 sts, k3

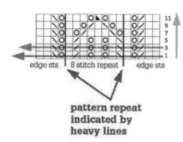

edge sts | 8 stitch repeat | edge sts

pattern repeat indicated by heavy lines

Row 1: k2, k2tog, yo, k1, *(edge stitches)* *then start repeating pattern:*
[ssk, k1, yo, k1, yo, k2tog, k1] repeat to last 4 sts,
yo, ssk, k2 *(edge sts)*

Row 2: (not shown on chart) ...
follow text instructions
k3, purl to last 3 sts, k3

Row 3: k2, k2tog, yo, k1, *(edge stitches)* *then start repeating pattern:*
[ssk, k1, yo, k1, yo, k2tog, k1] repeat to last 4 sts,
yo, ssk, k2 *(edge sts)*

and so on and so forth...

If the knitting chart shows both the 'right' and 'wrong' side of the knitting project, you will work the 'right side' instructions from right to left, and the 'wrong side' instructions from left to right. By looking at the chart as a picture of the finished cloth, it will start to make sense as you progress.

Designing Your Own

After working from patterns for a while, you make wish to design your own. Creating your very own product in exactly the way you'd like to is a huge and satisfying achievement and there are a lot of online resources for sharing your personalized knitting if you chose to share what you've created to help others. A great example of this can be found at website _allfreeknitting.com_.

When it comes to **designing your own pattern**, below is **a great checklist to work from**. If you follow the steps listed below, you will find designing a pattern and fun and simple task:

Initial sketches – start with a simple sketch of what you want to create. This may seem silly if you know what you want in your mind, but it'll give you a great reference point.

Yarn – now is the time to pick what type of yarn you want to work with. What texture and color do you want your finished product to be? You need to consider what is familiar to you and what will work with the stitches you intend to use.

Measurements – you need to work out how big you want the finished project to be. If it's a garment you need to get the body measurements for yourself – or whoever it is for – correct.

Gauge swatch – the gauge swatch will confirm the yarn and needle size and it'll ensure the finished project is the right size. You can test this out while drawing up your pattern.

Stitches – now is the time to start actually writing the pattern! Start by multiplying your gauge swatch by the size of the finished project. Once you have all the size measured up you can start figuring out all the stitches.

Write the pattern – now you have all the stitches figured out, you can get it all written out in a coherent manner using the abbreviations.

Knit – now you can work from the pattern you have created to knit the product you desire.

Critique – fix any errors you've discovered whilst knitting and have a think about what you'd change if you were to do it again. Then, you're ready to start all over again!

Here are four tips for getting your pattern exactly right:

- **_Gauge_** – knowing the gauge is vital to ensure knitters get the right size product at the end.

- **_Abbreviations_** – be sure to use the standard knitting abbreviations. If you have created your very own stitch, you'll need to have a key at the beginning of the pattern explaining exactly what its abbreviation means.

- **_Technique details_** – you need to consider beginners when writing your pattern. You'll always want to be very specific with technique details so that it can be understood by anyone.

- **_Organize the pattern_** – use sub-headings to tell users which part of the pattern they're working on. Especially if it's a larger project such as a sweater. 'Sleeves', 'Collar', etc will be useful.

This book is now going to look at how to complete a knitting project – with step-by-step guides for a lot of the basic stitches, techniques and tips and tricks to ensure that you have everything you need to complete basic patterns. Then there will be a selection of patterns for you to practice. By the time you have finished everything within the following chapters, moving on to harder patterns and learning new stitches will be easy for you!

EMMA BROWN

KNITTING PROJECTS

So now that you know how to read knitting patterns, it's time to look at everything you'll need to know to work a knitting project. You have the yarn, the needles and any other equipment listed in the pattern and all you have to do is begin.

Starting Knitting

The first thing you need to do is **cast/bind on** which is the terminology for *getting the yarn onto the needle*. Here is a useful step-by-step guide for the most commonly used cast on technique.

Slip Knot - Start by making a loop with the yarn.

Bring the yarn through the loop, creating another loop with a knot at the end

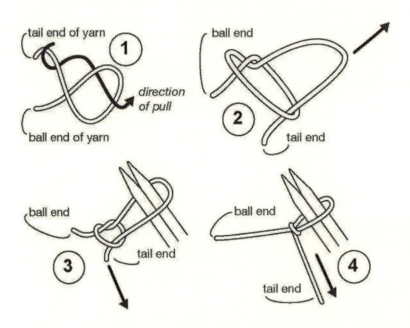

Cast On - After you have created the slip knot, you will need to cast on. This is effectively the first stitch to get you going. You may already know that this is something you need to do, but did you know that there are actually 4 different ways of doing this? Below demonstrates with step-by-step guides how to do this.

Single Cast On

1. Slide slip knot onto needle. Pull yarn to tighten knot.

2. Wrap the working yarn (yarn connected to the ball of yarn) around your thumb so you have a loop around your thumb.

3. Bring the needle under and up through the loop around your thumb.

4. Remove your thumb from the loop and pull the yarn.

5. Continue from step 2 until you have desired number of stitches casted on.

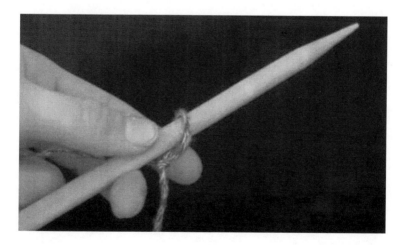

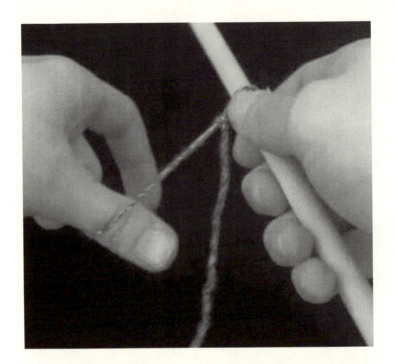

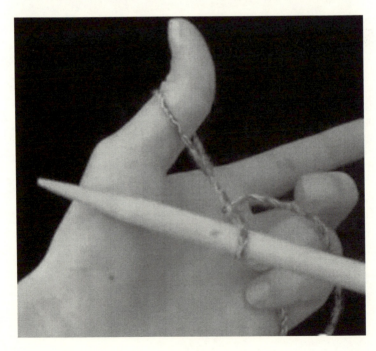

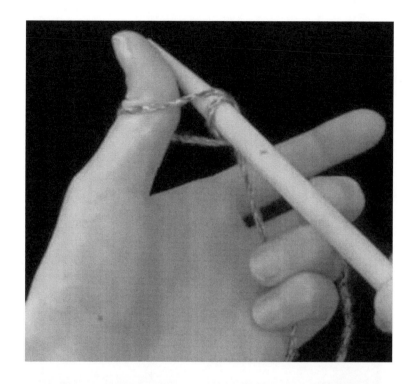

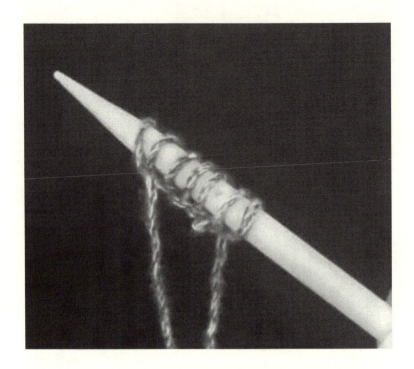

Longtail Cast On

Before you start to cast on, leave a tail at the end of the yarn. The length of the tail depends on the number of stitches you want to cast on. If you want to cast on 10 stitches leave about a foot of yarn for the tail.

1. Drape the tail over your thumb and pointer finger on your left hand.

2. Catch it in between your pointer and middle finger.

3. Catch the yarn connected to the ball against your palm with your pinky and ring fingers.

4. Take the needle in your right hand. Place it on top of the yarn between your thumb and pointer finger.

5. Draw the yarn towards you with the needle. You should see a loop of yarn around your thumb.

6. Bring the needle under the outer piece of yarn next to your thumb and up through the loop.

7. Bring the needle back towards your pointer finger.

8. Bring the needle over the yarn connected to your pointer finger and then under back towards the thumb.

9. Drop the head of the needle back down through the loop around your thumb.

10. Release your thumb from the loop and pull the yarn.

11. Repeat from step 6 until you have the desired number of stitches casted on.

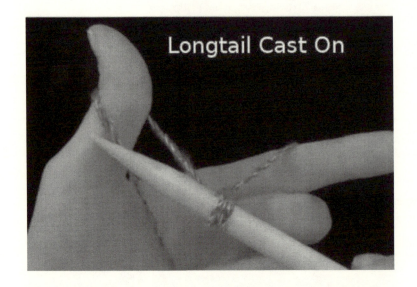

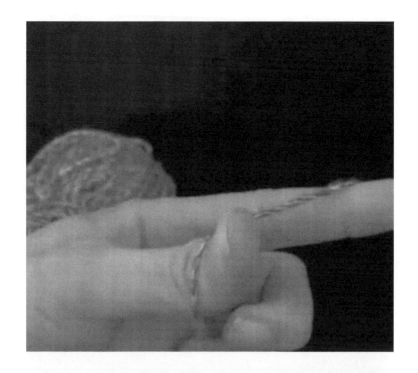

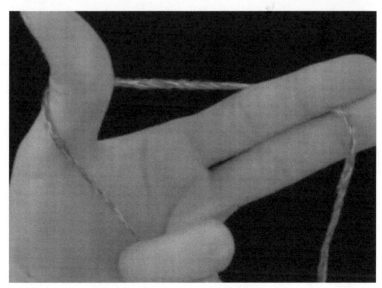

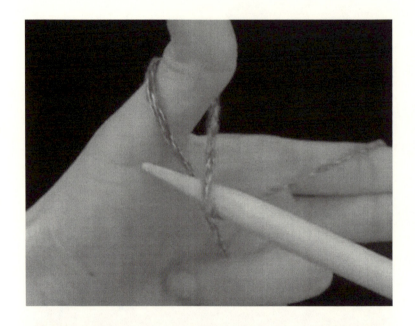

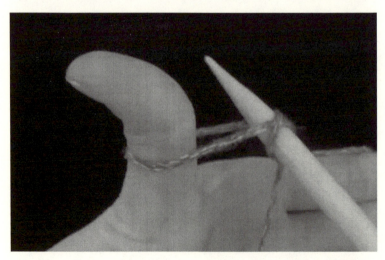

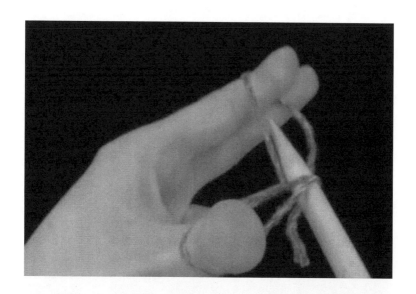

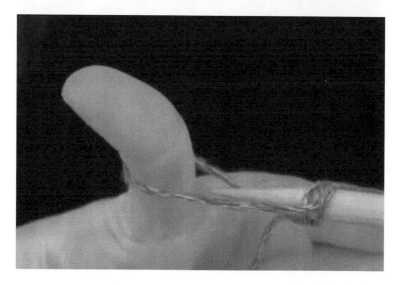

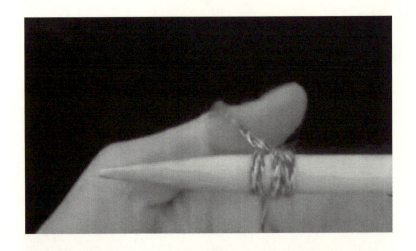

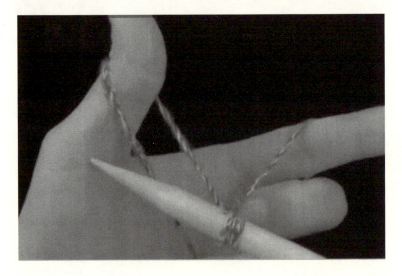

Knit Cast On

1. Make a slip knot and put it on your needle. Hold this needle in your left hand and take the second needle in your right hand.

2. Pass the needle in the right hand through the loop on the left needle and bring the right needle under the left needle.

3. With your left hand, wrap the working yarn around your left hand needle.

4. Bring the right needle back through the loop on the left needle.

5. Now you have a loop around your right needle. Turn the loop and drop it on to the left needle and release the right needle from the loop.

6. Pull the yarn and you have two stitches casted on.

7. To continue, repeat from step 2.

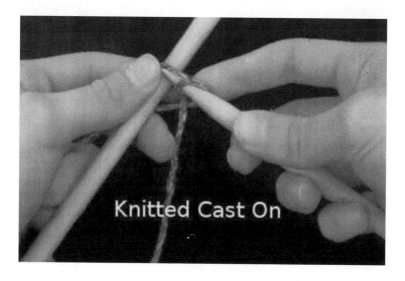

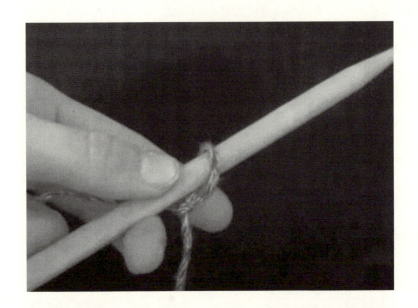

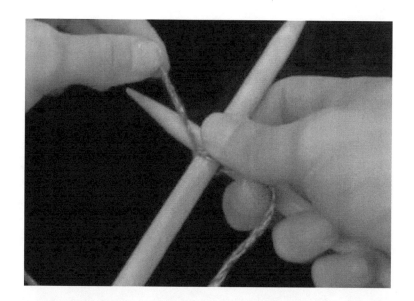

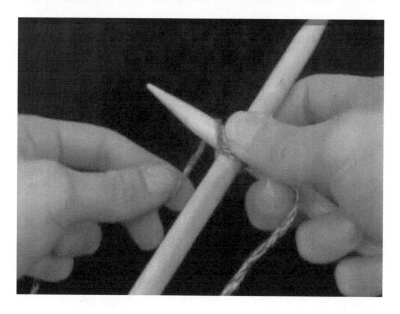

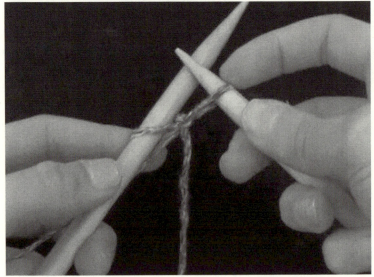

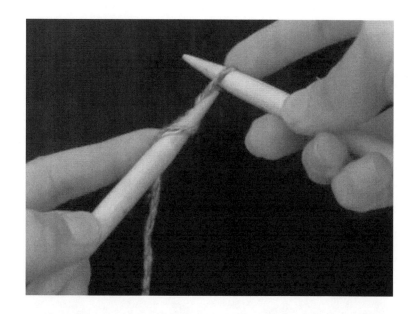

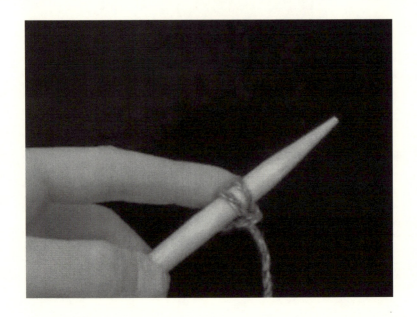

Cable Cast On

1. For the first two stitches, use instructions for knitted cast on.

2. Once you have two stitches casted on. Take your right needle and put it in between the two stitches by bringing it under the left needle and through the yarn that connects the two stitches.

3. Wrap the working yarn around the right needle.

4. Bring the right needle back through the loops.

5. Now you have a loop around your right needle. Turn the loop and drop it on to the left needle and release the right needle from the loop.

6. Pull the yarn. You should have two stitches casted on. To continue, repeat from step 2.

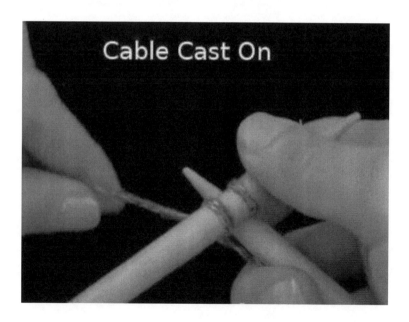

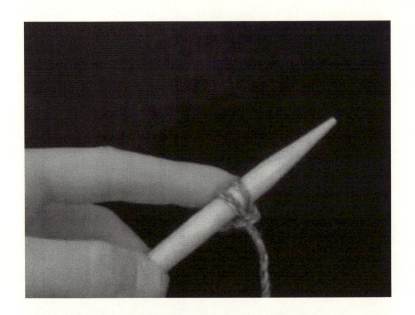

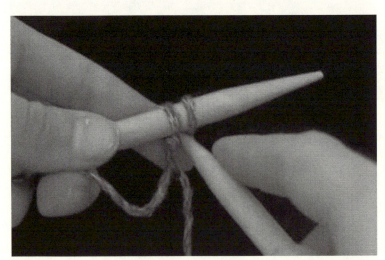

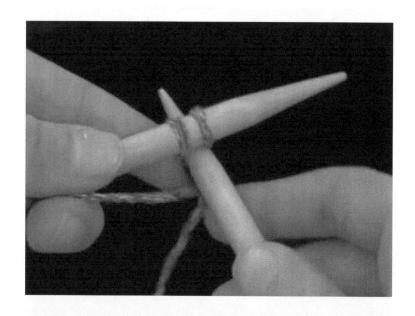

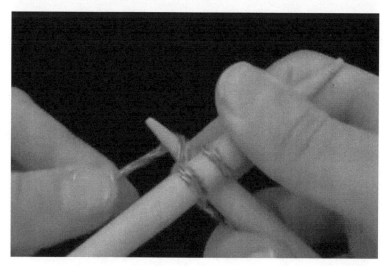

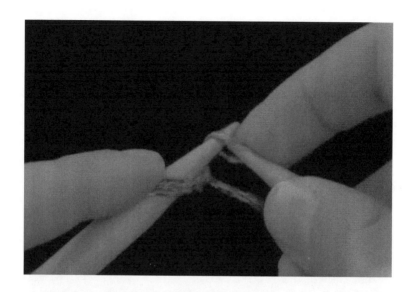

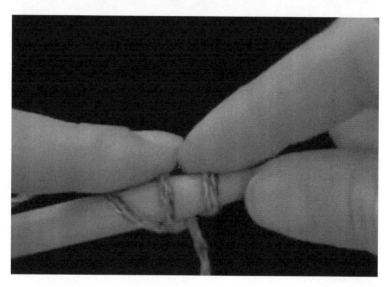

Knitting Gauge

Knitting a gauge swatch is **so important** as it helps you determine if the equipment you're using to knit with will create an end project that is the size you desire. **Missing out this step can result in the whole project coming out entirely the wrong size**.

To complete the gauge, follow these steps:

Stitches – cast on the stitches required. It is normally 4 inches, plus 6 more stitches. So, for example if the gauge is given as 18 stitches and 22 rows over 4 inches, cast on 24 stitches.

Rows – work in the stitch pattern specified for the number of rows requires to make 4 inches, plus 6 rows. Using the gauge specifications from the example above (18 stitches and 22 rows over 4 inches), you work in the given pattern of 28 rows.

Bind Off – finish the project and bind off loosely, cut the yarn leaving an 8 inch tail.

Measure – you'll then want to measure the swatch to check the right number of stitches create the right size swatch. If not, you will need to change the needle size or yarn or the end result will be wrong. If you need more stitches per inch, you need smaller needles or thinner yarn and if you need less stitches per inch, you'll want to change to bigger needles or thicker yarn.

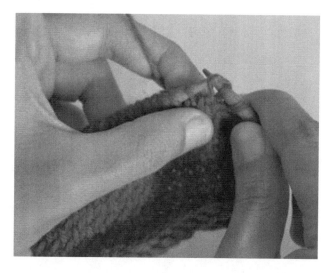

Flat Knitting

Flat knitting is **the process of knitting in rows, where you periodically turn the work.** There is a '*right side*' and a '*wrong side*' of the project. Once you have Cast On, you immediately start to knit the next row from the pattern.

Here is a guide to start flat knitting:

Step 1: Place your right needle behind the left needle.

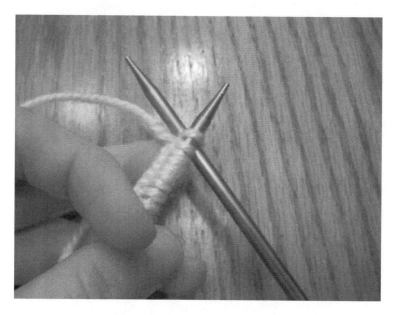

Step 2: Wrap the yarn counter clockwise around the right needle, and behind the left needle.

Step 3: Pull the yarn through the loop so it is on the right needle (like above).

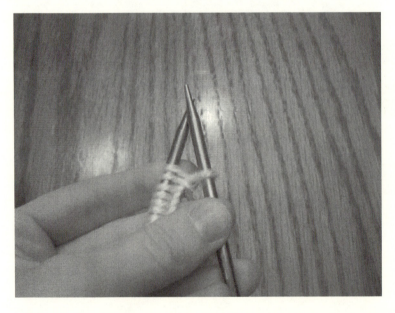

Step 4: Here's where it gets different. Push the first stitch on the left needle off of the needle completely.

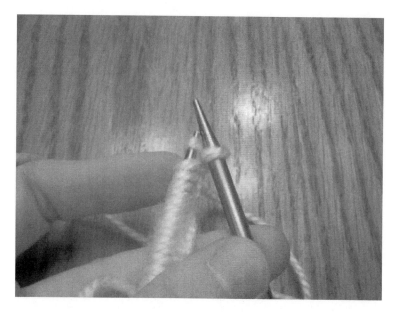

Step 5: Now you'll have less stitches on the left needle, and one on the right.

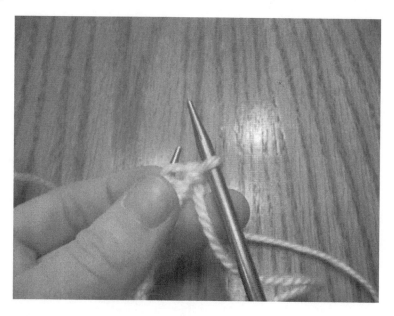

Step 6: Continue this same method down the row.

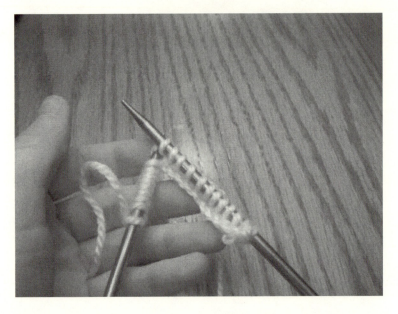

Step 7: Once all of the stitches are off of the left needle and on the right needle, that row is done.

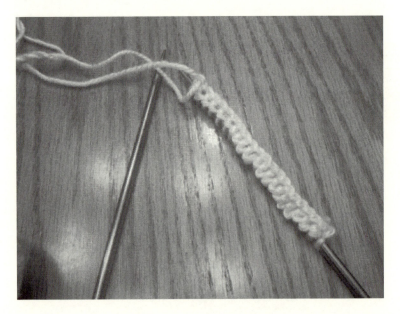

Step 8: For the next row, move what was your right needle to your left hand now, and your left needle to your right hand (flip them). The needle with the stitches on it will always start off in your left hand.

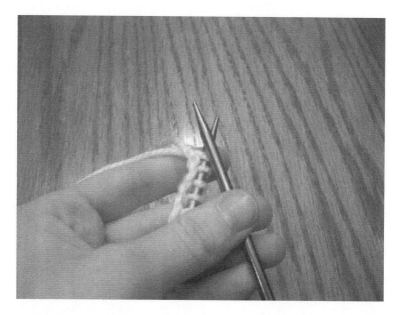

Step 9: Continue stitching the next row as you did the first.

Step 10: When you have the next row done, you will begin to see the pattern forming.

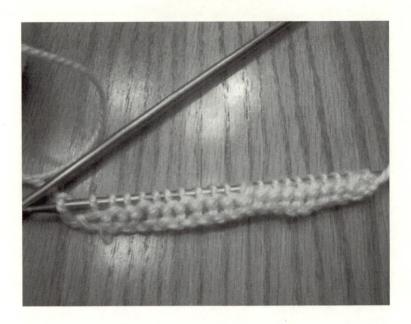

Circular Knitting

Circular knitting – or **knitting in the round** – is a **form of knitting that creates a seamless tube**. Using circular knitting needles, the yarn is cast on and the circle of stitches is joined. This type of knitting is perfect for creating socks, mittens or bigger projects such as sweaters.

Here is a step-by-step guide for this type of knitting:

If you don't join the ends, you can use your circular needle to knit flat pieces, just like you'd knit on conventional needles. Because of the long connector between the needles, you can knit large items like afghans and not have to join then.

You can also knit in the round on your circular needles. When you do, you'll find that the right side of the work is facing towards you, which can make patterns easy to see.

You cast on to your circular needle in exactly the same way that you cast onto straight needles.

Continue to cast on until you have the number of stitches required for your pattern. You'll find that the circular needle is now full.

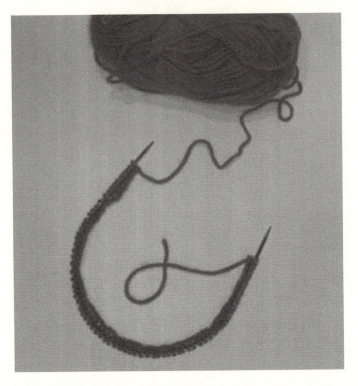

It is extremely important when joining your work that it is not twisted around the needle! If your piece is twisted, you will end up having to rip it out. To join, hold your needle so that the yarn is coming from the right. When you are knitting in the round, it is a good idea to use a stitch marker to know where your piece began - slip one onto your needle now if you will be using one. Place your knitting on a flat surface and carefully turn your cast-on stitches so that they are all facing in the same way (in our example, they are facing to the bottom and inside of the needle.)

Then insert the right needle into the first stitch that you cast on and knit the stitch. Be sure to pull the first stitches tight so you don't get a gap where the rounds join.

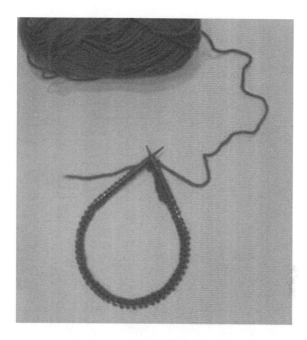

Continue to knit – you'll find that the 'right' side is always on the outside
and that, as your work grows, that patterns are easy to see!

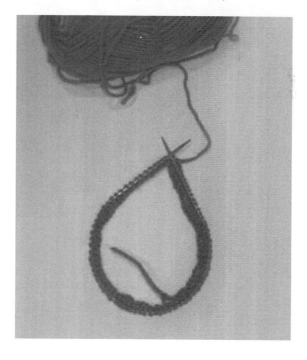

Finishing

You have to Cast/Bind Off your knitting properly to prevent your work from unraveling. Below is a great step-by-step guide for doing this in the most effective way possible:

Step 1: Knit the first 2 stitches of the row.

Step 2: Insert the left needle into the first stitch on the right needle.

Step 3: Pull the first stitch on the right needle over the second stitch and off the right needle. The second stitch will now be the only stitch on the right needle.

Step 4: Knit the next stitch on the left needle so that there are now 2 stitches on the right needle.

Repeat steps 2 and 3 until the end of the row.

When all stitches in the row have been bound off, cut a tail at least 4" long (or as long as the pattern specifies) and pull this tail through the last stitch, pulling to secure the work.

STITCHES

Now that you know how to start and finish a knitting project on top of the flat knitting stitches, **it is time to learn some of the other stitches** that you will come across in knitting patterns. Practicing them using these step-by-step guides will make them so much easier to complete when you need to.

Basic

1. The Purl Stitch

The Purl Stitch is generally the second stitch that knitters learn. It's primarily thought of as a **backwards stitch**. Always remember to keep the working yarn in front of your needles. If you're switching between knit and purl stitches, you will move your working yarn from the back of the work to the front of the work, between the needles, to prepare for a purl stitch.

Step 1: You must first cast on or pick up stitches to have a foundation of stitches on your left needle.

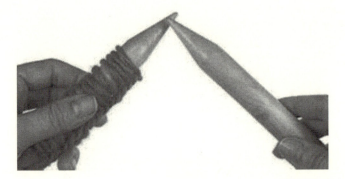

Step 2: Holding your working yarn to the front and keeping yarn tensioned over your left index finger, insert the needle from back to front through the first loop on the needle. Keep the left needle under the right needle and the yarn to the front of the work. With your left index finger, bring the working yarn over the top to the bottom over the right needle to create a loop.

Step 3: Pull the loop on the right needle back out through the stitch on the left needle.

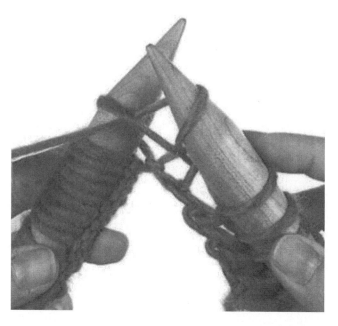

Step 4: Moving your right needle, slip the stitch off of the left needle. This completes a purl stitch. Continue to make as many purl stitches in the row as desired.

2. Knit to Purl

Knit to Purl stitches create a rib effect which looks amazing and I very often used for garments such as cardigans.

After the purl stitch, the yarn is at the front of the work

Take the yarn to the back of the work between the needles

It's easy to recognize which is the purl and which is the knit stitch. The purl stitches have a horizontal bar (a small bump) under the stitch on the needle, whereas the knit stitches do not.

3. Eyelet Stitches

Eyelet stitches are a simple technique which produces beautiful results. It is effectively a small hole in the fabric which can either be purely for decoration, or for threading something through – like ribbon.

Here is a great *guide for creating a basic eyelet stitch pattern*:

- Knit one row at the length you desire.

- Purl the next row.

- Moving onto the third row, knit two stitches.

- Then yarn over, knit two stitches together, knit one stitch.

- Repeat the steps in the point above until the end of the row.

- Purl the next row.

- Repeat all of these steps until the eyelet stitch is complete.

A visual step-by-step is shown below:

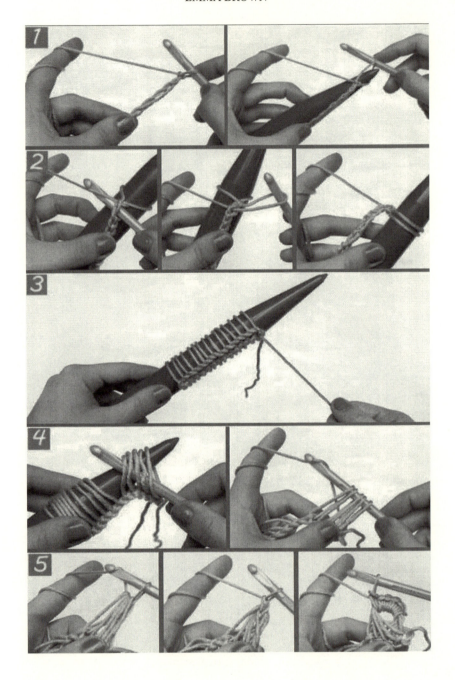

4. Twist Stitch

Twisted stitches produce mini-cables and create a beautifully unique effect that will make your knitting appear very professional. You can twist left or right, as shown below.

Twist Left

This will feel like working an ssk decrease. First, twist 1 over 1 left.

Slip first stitch, knitwise.

Slip second stitch, knitwise.

Insert left-hand needle through the 2 stitches, as if working an ssk decrease

Slip the 2 stitches together back to the left-hand needle in this manner, twisting them so their order is reversed

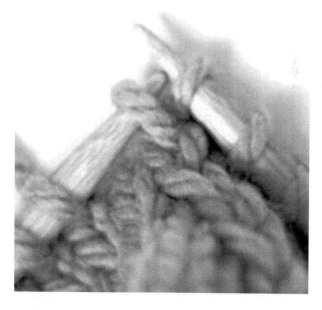

Knit (or purl) the first stitch, which is the back stitch.

Knit the second stitch, which is the front stitch.

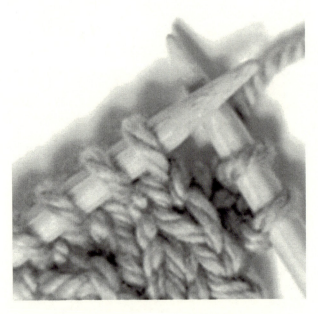

Now, twist 1 over 2 stitches left, using the same method but with 3stitches total instead of 2.

Slip the next 3 stitches knitwise, one at a time.

Insert the left-hand needle through the 3 slipped stitches, as if working an sssk double-decrease.

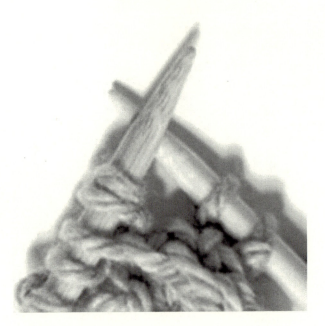

Slip the stitches back onto the left-hand needle, then knit (or purl) all 3 - the first 2 are the back stitches, the third is the front stitch.

Twist Right

First, twist 1 over 1 right. Insert right-hand needle through next 2 stitches knitwise, together as if to knit 2 together.

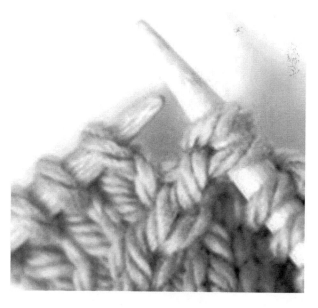

Slip those stitches onto the right-hand needle this way.

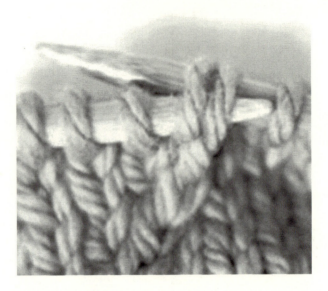

Insert the left-hand needle through the 2 slipped stitches, straight through, so needles are positioned as if slipping purlwise.

Now stitches are on the left-hand needle in the correct twisted order, they have become twisted (the other meaning of twisted, the individual knit loops are on the needle the wrong way)

Knit the first stitch through the back loop, which will untwist it – this is the top stitch.

Knit (or purl) the second stitch - this is the back stitch; if knitting it through the back loop to untwist it, if purling, it's not necessary to purl backwards as the purl bump will hide the twist.

Now, twist 1 over 2 stitches right, using the same method but with 3 stitches total instead of 2 - start by slipping 3 as if knitting 3 together.

Slip the 3 stitches back to the left-hand needle, straight across so needles are

positioned as if slipping purlwise

Knit (or purl) the 3 stitches, knitting through back loops to untwist the first stitch is the front stitch, the second and third are the back stitches.

5. Moss Stitch

The moss stitch – sometimes known as a **_seed stitch_** – is an easy to create stitch, which produces wonderfully complex looking results. Follow directions for how to complete a moss stitch pattern below.

The Moss or Seed stitch consists of single knits and purls that alternate horizontally and vertically. Like the garter stitch, the moss stitch lies flat, making it a good edging for a sweater border and cuffs. The knitted fabric also looks the same from both sides, making it a nice choice for scarves and other pieces of which both sides are visible.

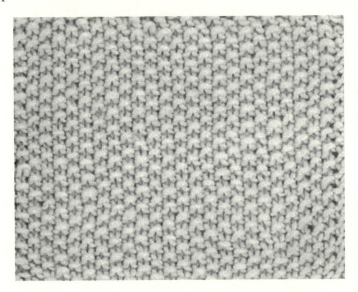

Cast on an even number of stitches.

Row 1: Alternate between knitting 1 stitch and purling 1 stitch across the row.

Row 2: Alternate between purling 1 stitch and knitting 1 stitch across the row.

Repeat Rows 1 and 2 for pattern.

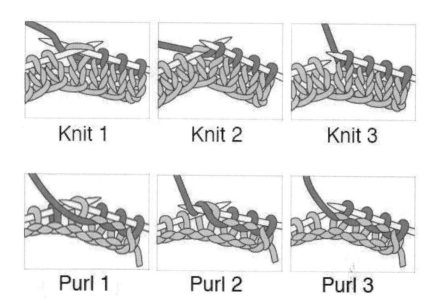

Knit 1   Knit 2   Knit 3

Purl 1   Purl 2   Purl 3

When working the moss or seed stitch, you alternate between knit and purl stitches in each row. The trick to creating the little "seeds" is to knit in the purl stitches of the previous row and purl in the knit stitches of the previous row.

6. Garter Stitch

The garter stitch is often used to create scarves and blankets because it produces a sturdy material that doesn't roll at the edges.

To knit the garter stitch, hold the yarn in your right hand, and hold the knitting needle with the cast-on stitches in your left hand (with the tip pointing to the right). Make sure that the first stitch is no more than 1 inch from the tip of the needle.

Insert the tip of the empty (right hand) needle into the first stitch on the left hand needle from left to right and front to back, forming a T shape with the tips of the needles. The right hand needle will be behind the left hand needle.

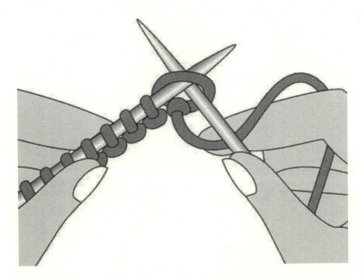

With your right hand, bring the yarn to the front from the left side of the right hand needle, and then over the right hand needle to the right and down between the needles.

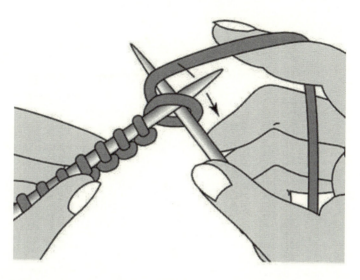

You can try to maneuver the yarn with your right forefinger or just hold it between your thumb and forefinger for now. Keeping a slight tension on the wrapped yarn, bring the tip of the right hand needle with its wrap of yarn through the loop on the left hand needle to the front.

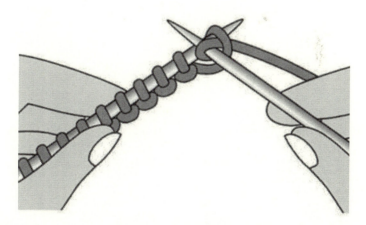

The right hand needle is now in front of the left hand needle. Keep the tip of the left forefinger on the point of the right hand needle to help guide the needle through the old stitch and prevent losing the wrap of yarn. Slide the right needle to the right until the old loop on the left hand needle drops off.

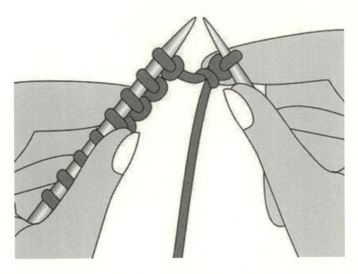

You now have a new stitch/loop on the right hand needle — the old stitch hangs below it. Then you need to repeat steps 1 through 4 until you've knitted all the stitches from your left hand needle.

Your left hand needle is now empty, and your right hand needle is full of new stitches. Turn your work (that is, switch hands so that the needle with stitches is in your left hand) and knit the new row.

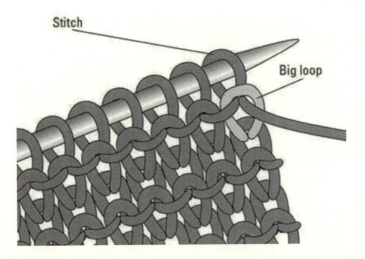

When you turn your work, the yarn strand coming out of the first stitch to knit is hanging down in the front. The stitch just below the first stitch (big loop) on your left hand needle is larger than the rest and can obscure your view of where your needle should go. To better see the opening of the first stitch, keep the strand in front and gently pull down on it, and the big loop if necessary. Be sure to insert the point of the right hand needle into the loop on the left hand needle and not into the stitch below. Repeat all as necessary.

7. Rib Stitch

The ribbing stitch looks great whether it's done in one block solid color, or a few colors. It's often used to create afghans, scarves and garments.

The ribbing stitch uses two stitches – a knit stitch and a purl stitch. Start by knitting two stitches. Bring the yarn from the back of your work between the needles to the front. Now purl two stitches. Bring the yarn to the back of your work between the needles. Knit two stitches. Continue to knit two stitches, purl two stitches until you reach the end of the row or until the pattern instructs you to do something different.

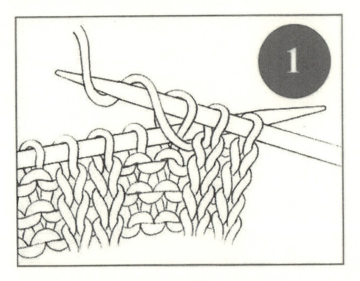

On subsequent rows, knit the knit stitches (V stitches) and purl the purl stitches (bump stitches) Remember to have the working yarn in BACK when you knit and in FRONT when you purl.

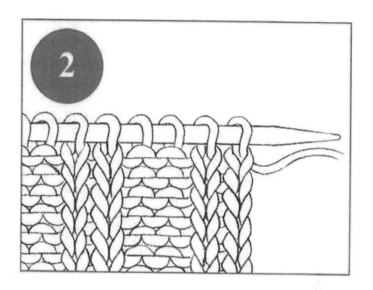

8. Basketweave Stitch

The basketweave stitch produces a beautiful fabric that appears woven. Despite its complex appearance, it's actually very easy to complete, as shown below.

Cast on a multiple of 8 stitches, plus 5 stitches.

Rows 1 and 5 (RS): Knit across.

Rows 2 and 4: Knit 5, then purl 3 and knit 5 alternately until the end of the row.

Row 3: Purl 5, then knit 3 and purl 5 alternately until the end of the row.

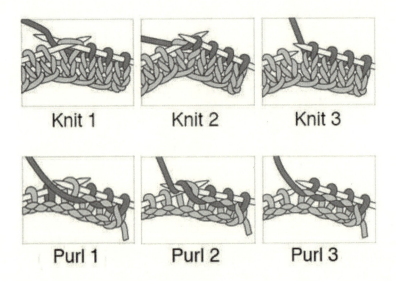

Rows 6 and 8: Knit 1, purl 3, then knit 5, purl 3 until the last stitch, knit 1.

Row 7: Purl 1, knit 3, then purl 5 and knit 3 alternately until the last stitch, knit 1.

Repeat Rows 1–8 until desired length.

9. Drop Stitch

A dropped stitch will happen to every knitter at some point in forever. Usually it's a mistake, but there are instances you'll actually want to do it on purpose because it can produce some really unusual effects, as shown by the guide below.

Dropping stitches is an act most of us have done without even trying: it happens when a stitch falls from your needle and creates a run in the fabric. When you don't want it to happen, your best bet is to use a crochet hook to hook the stitches back up onto your needle. However, sometimes you may want to drop stitches on purpose to create an easy-to-work lacy knitted fabric. Here's how:

Step 1: Knit (or purl) until you reach the stitch you'd like to drop.

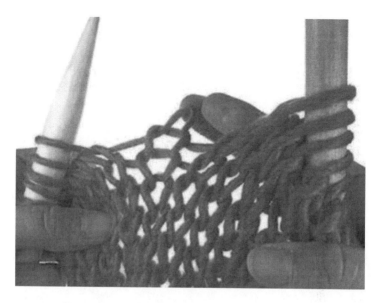

Step 2: Grab the stitch off the needle.

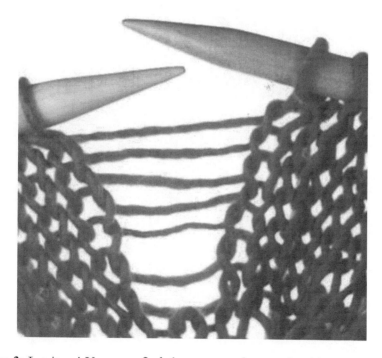

Step 3: Let it go! You may find that you need to work a bit at unraveling the stitches.

10. Border Stitch

There are many things you might want to add a border or edging too – a scarf, an afghan or even some garments. There are a few ways you can do this, including the method shown below.

Begin by casting on the number of stitches needed for the border. Here, the body yarn (mauve) has been attached to the border yarn (gray) by way of a simple overhand knot. If you want, you can undo this knot later and weave in the ends. But if you were doing the border in the same yarn as the body, then you wouldn't even need to attach anything, just continue with the same yarn.

Work in border pattern until you have one stitch left from the border and one stitch left from the body. Here you can clearly see them – one gray, one mauve. And work a joining decrease using one border and one body stitch. This joining decrease has 2 purposes. 1. It attaches the border-in-progress to the body, and 2. It anchors the body stitch so that it will not unravel. It's like binding it off, but without involving any other body stitches.

After working a joining decrease, you will turn the piece and work the next border row. But in order to give a flat join and minimize bulk, it's best to slip the first border stitch (which is the stitch that you just created by working the joining decrease). The stitch to be slipped is the first border stitch closest to the body stitches.

If you continue in this fashion, joining every other border row to the body via a joining decrease, you will begin to see how the border is attached.

This is an alternate view of the same point, where you can see the way the body and the border stitches twist together to form the joining decrease.

Continue with the border rows until all of the body stitches are used up. It's preferable to finish with a joining row. Then work the final row, binding off as you go, until you have one body and one border stitch left, then work my joining decrease and bind off the final stitch. As you can see, the edge lies flat and even this way.

In this close-up you can see how the body rows (mauve) are worked horizontally, and the border rows (gray) are worked vertically.

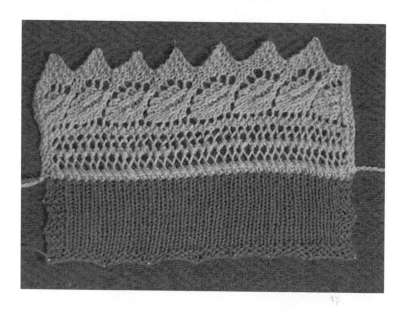

Advanced

11. The Bobble Stitch

Bobbles are a cool addition to a knitting project that can make a basic project or garment look spectacular. They're more complex than any of the stitches we've looked at so far, but the practice you've put into them will put you at a higher ability level.

To create a bobble you rapidly increase into a single stitch, work these stitches for two or more rows and then decrease them back to one stitch.

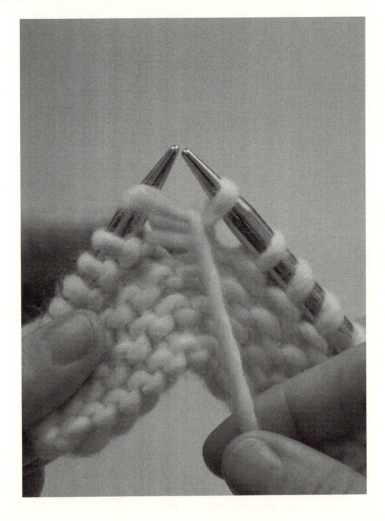

With the right side facing you, knit into the stitch where you'd like your bobble, keeping the stitch on the left needle, yarn over and knit into the same stitch again, yarn over and knit into the stitch for a third time.

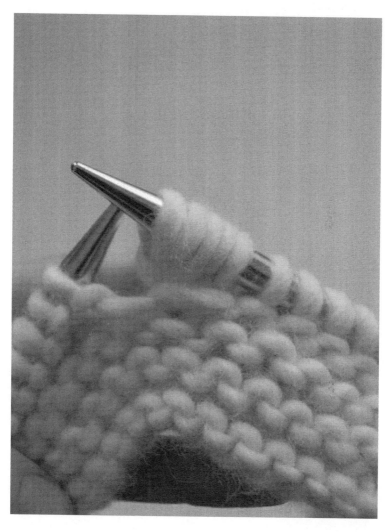

You now have 5 stitches where you initially had one.

Turn the work so the wrong side is facing you.

Knit the 5 bobble stitches.

Turn the work so the right side is facing you. Knit the first two bobble stitches together. Place this stitch back onto the left needle.

Pass the remaining three stitches, one at a time, over the knit-together stitch and off the needle, as if to bind off.

Knit the remaining bobble stitch, returning it to the right needle.

12. Leaf Stitch

This pattern is extremely fancy to look at and is often used to make garments look more professional. Here's a brilliant step-by-step guide that shows you how to knit a leaf stitch:

Cast on 17 stitches, then knit across the first row.

Row 2: P1, *K6, P3, K6, p1; repeat from * across.

Row 3: *K8, yarn over, K1, yarn over, K7; repeat from * to last stitch, K1 to end.

Row 4: P1, *K6, P5, K6, P1; repeat from * across.

Row 5: *K9, yarn over, K1, yarn over, K8; repeat from * to last stitch, K1 to end.

Row 6: P1, *K6, P7, K6, P1; repeat from * across.

Row 7: *K10, yarn over, K1, yarn over, K9; repeat from * to last stitch, K1 to end.

Row 8: P1, *K6, P9, K6, P1; repeat from * across.

Row 9: *K11, yarn over, K1, yarn over, K10; repeat from * to last stitch, K1 to end.

Row 10: P1, *K6, P11, K6, P1; repeat from * across.

Increase Rows.

Row 11: *K7, Slip Slip Knit(ssk), K7, Knit 2 together, K6; repeat from * to last stitch, K1 to end.

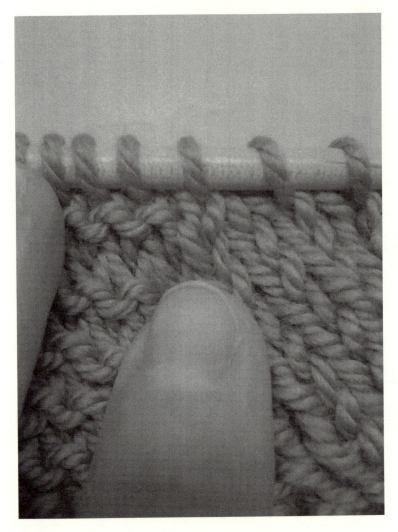

Row 12: P1, *K6, P9, K6, P1; repeat from * across.

Row 13: *K7, ssk, K5, k2tog, K6; repeat from * to last stitch, K1 to end.

Row 14: P1, *K6, P7, K6, P1; repeat from * across.

Row 15: *K7, ssk, K3, k2tog, K6; repeat from * to last stitch, K1 to end.

Row 16: P1, *K6, P5, K6, P1; repeat from * across.

Row 17: *K7, ssk, K1, k2tog, K6; repeat from * to last stitch, K1 to end.

Row 18: P1, *K6, P3, K6, P1; repeat from * across.

Row 19: *K7, k3tog, K6; repeat from * to last stitch, K1 to end.

Row 20: P1; *K6, P1; repeat from * across.

Row 21: *K7, Knit in front and back and front again, K6; repeat from * to last stitch, K1 to end.

13. Trinity Stitch

The trinity stitch produces a textured fabric. It's a more advanced stitch, but it's still very achievable.

Cast on a multiple of 4 stitches, plus 2 stitches.

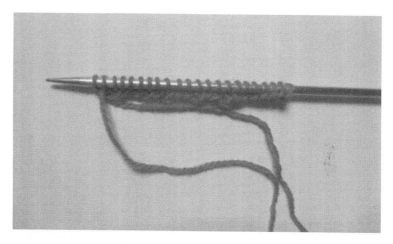

For the first row, knit the first stitch. Knit the second stitch, but don't drop it from the left needle right away.

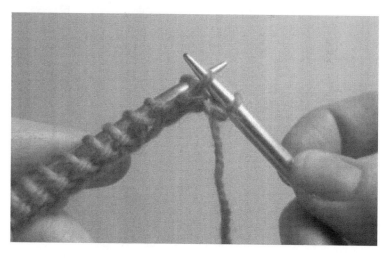

Now you need to purl into that same stitch. In order to do that, you need to bring your yarn to the front.

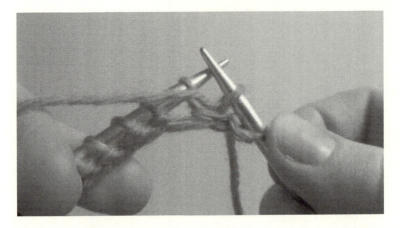

The purl as you normally would – don't drop the stitch from your left needle yet.

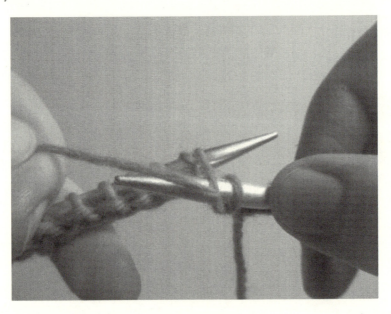

Bring your yarn to the back of your work in preparation for another knit stitch.

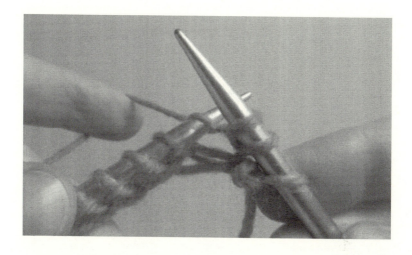

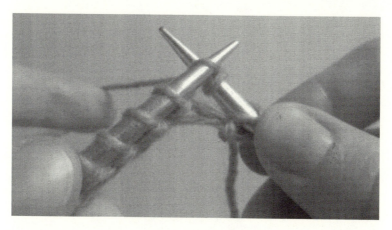

Knit, then drop the stitch from the needle.

Purl 3 stitches together.

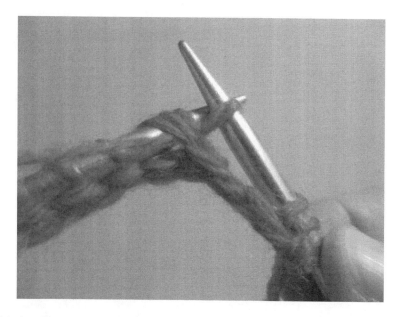

This is what your yarn will look like after you complete the set of stitches listed above.

Repeat the stitches listed above across the row. When you get to the last stitch, knit one. At the end of the row, your piece will look like this:

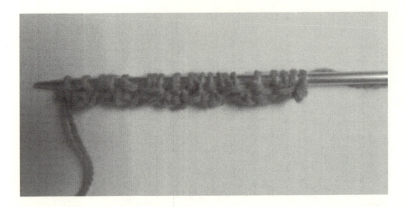

For the next row, purl right across.

The third row is the same to the first, except you work in reverse.

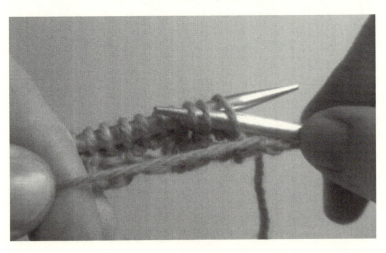

Purl 3 stitches together. Then you need to K1, P1, K1 as you did in the first row. Be sure to bring the yarn to the front to purl, and take it to the back to knit. Repeat this process until the end of the row. Repeat the 4 rows of the trinity stitch until the desired length.

14. Loop Stitch

The loop stitch is a quirky technique that produces a very unique result. This makes scarves, bags, even garments that stand out! A great guide to create the loop stitch is presented below.

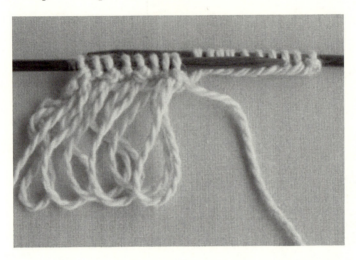

When knitting loops, they will form on the back side of the row you're working on. To start with, insert the left needle into the stitch you want to make the loop in, and wind the yarn around the needle, as if to knit.

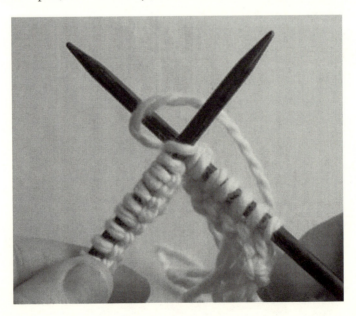

Wind the yarn around your left index finger. If you want a short loop do this once, for longer, do it twice.

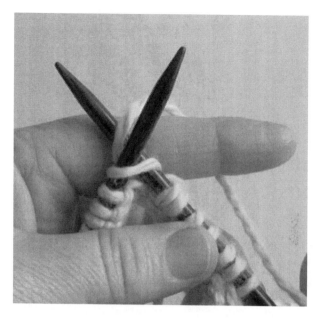

Take the yarn back around the right needle as if to knit again, and form the stitch. It will be 2 or 3 strands wide depending on how many times you have the yarn wrapped around your finger.

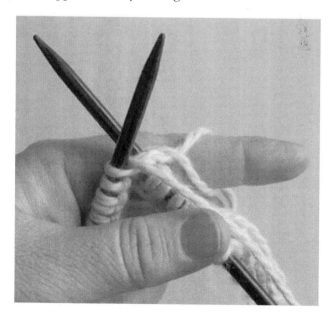

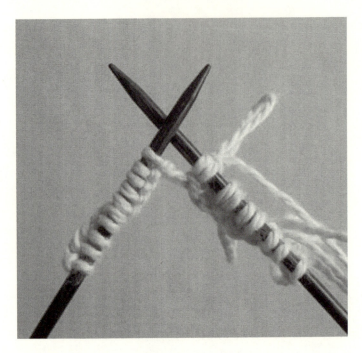

To secure the loop, bring the working yarn between the needles to the front of the work, then over the needles in the same way you'd work a yarn over.

Hold the yarn over securely in place and bind off the stitch over the yarn over. This will secure the loop.

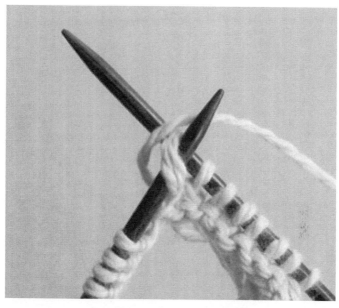

15. Shell Stitch

The shell stitch is often seen on knitted afghans because it looks brilliant in one color, or in multiple.

Cast on a multiple of 7 stitches, plus an extra 2. Then knit the first row.

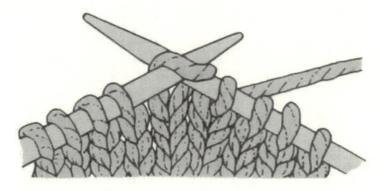

Purl the second row.

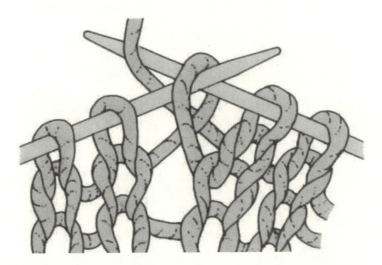

For the third row, you'll need to knit 2 stitches, then yarn over. Then you will want to purl one stitch, then purl 3 more together, purl on again, yarn over and knit 2:

Row 3: K2 *YO, P1, P3tog, P1, YO, K2*

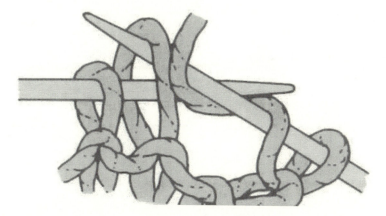

Purl the fourth row. Repeat these four rows until the knitted piece is the length you desire.

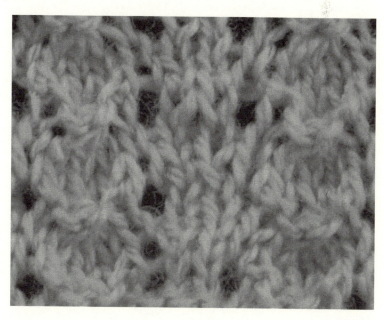

16. Slip Stitch

A stitch is slipped by passing it from one needle to the other without working it. It's done when decreasing, adding in color or making a specific pattern. This is primarily done purlwise as it leaves a smoother result so only perform a slip stitch knitwise if it is specified.

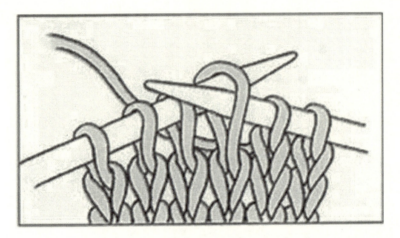

To slip a stitch purlwise, insert the right needle (from back to front) into the next stitch on the left needle and place it on the right needle without working it.

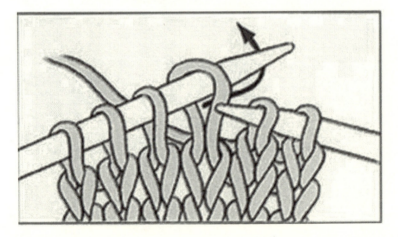

To slip a stitch knitwise, insert the right needle into the next stitch on the left needle as shown and place it on the right needle without working it.

17. Roman Stitch

The roman stitch is another more advanced stitch that is actually very simple to complete, but the end result appears extremely complex. It consists of 8 rows which can be repeated as necessary. A guide below shows you exactly what you need to do.

Cast on an even number of stitches. Knit the first row, then purl the second. The third and fourth rows consist of knitting 1 and purling one alternately for the entire row.

The fifth row is then knitted and the sixth purled. The seventh and eighth rows are one stitch purled, one knitted alternately through the whole row.

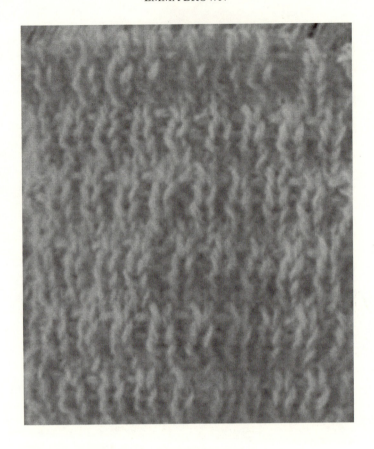

18. Linen Stitch

There are many variations to the linen stitch which can make a huge impact to how the end result looks.

The linen stitch is created by following the pattern listed below. This must be worked over an even number of stitches and all slipped stitches must be done purlwise.

Row 1: *Knit 1, slip 1 with yarn in front* Repeat * to * until the end of the row, then turn.

Row 2: *Purl 1, slip 1 with yarn in the back* Repeat * to * until the end of the row, then turn

For the two color pattern, work 2 rows in color A, then 2 in color B. Alternate in this way throughout the entire pattern until you have a result similar to what is shown below:

To add in a third color, you will want to work the linen pattern stitch in the following way:

Row 1: Color A

Row 2: Color B

Row 1: Color C

Row 2: Color A

Row 1: Color B

Row 2: Color C

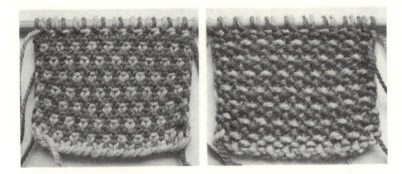

You can also work the linen stitch in the round using circular needles. When doing this, ensure that the right side of the fabric is always facing you. This means the pattern is slightly altered, but it is still worked over an even number of stitches:

Row 1: *Knit 1, slip 1 with yarn in front* Repeat * to * around.

Row 2: *Slip 1 with yarn in front, knit 1* Repeat * to * around.

19. Zig Zag Stitch

The Zig Zag pattern has become increasingly popular over the past few years because the effect is produces looks amazing in whatever style, pattern and color choice you go with.

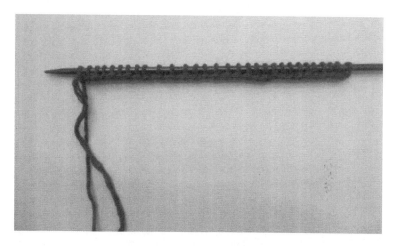

The first row (and all alternate odd-numbered rows) is purled right across.

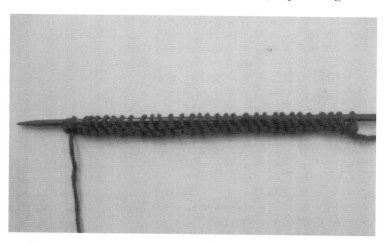

Then for the second row, knit the first stitch. Knit into the front and back of the next stitch. To do this, knit the stitch as you normally would but don't drop it off the left needle.

Stick your needle into the back of the same stitch you just knit.

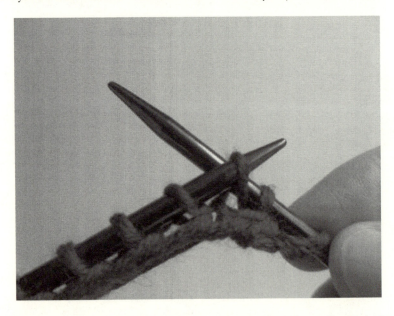

Knit into the back of the stitch and drop it from the left needle. Knit 4, slip a stitch – just remember, doing this causes a decrease in stitches and makes them lean to the left.

Knit 2 stitches together. This decreases stitches and makes them lean to the right. Combined with the slipped stitch, the chevron will be created.

Repeat all of the steps listed above until you have reached the desired length.

20. Herringbone Stitch

The herringbone stitch gives a chevron style finish, but the way it's knitted is very different, as explained by the guide below.

Cast on a multiple of 7 stitches, plus 1. The first and third rows are purled right across.

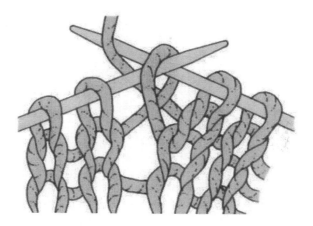

Row 2: *Knit 2 together, knit 2, place the point of the right-hand needle behind the left-hand needle and put the point of the right-hand needle through the top of the stitch below the stitch on the needle, from the top down, and knit, then knit the stitch above; knit 2. Repeat from * across, ending knit 1.

Row 4: Knit 1, *knit 2, increase as indicated above, knit 2, knit 2 together. Repeat from * across.

Repeat these rows for pattern.

KNITTING TECHNIQUES

There **are a few knitting techniques that are good for you to know.**
Mastering these will make the skill much easier to get to grips with.

1. Joining Yarn

At some point in your knitting, you will need to add a new ball of yarn. If you're completing a large project, it's likely you will need more than one ball. This demonstration on how to do this:

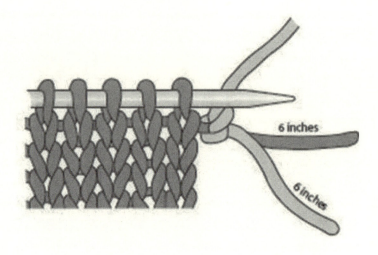

Step 1: Work a couple of stitches in from the end of your project. Leave 12 – 18 inches of your tail.

Step 2: Take the tail of the new ball of yarn and hold it with the tail from your project. Make sure the tails are going opposite directions from each other.

Step 3: Work a few more stitches holding both strands of yarn together.

Step 4: Continue working with the new strand, leaving 6 – 8 inches of your old tail

Note: Be careful to work both strand together as one during the next row.

When you ready, weave both tails into the project.

2. Increase & Decrease

Some knitting patterns require you to increase or decrease stitches to change the width of your knitting. Increasing is adding in a stitch, decreasing is taking one out. Below are a few ways to do this:

Increase Stitches

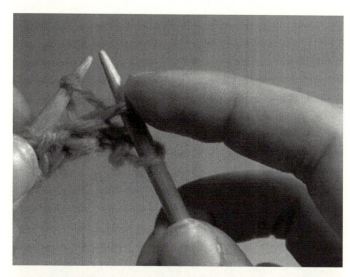

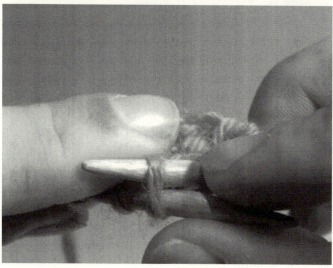

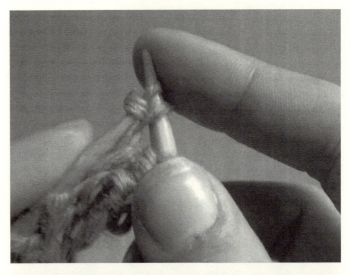

Increase Stitch: Basically, you are knitting two stitches like normal, but the first time you knit a stitch you do not slip the stitch off the left needle.

- Knit a stitch, but don't slip the stitch off your left needle

- Instead, bring your right needle through the top stitch on your left needle, and knit another stitch.

- Now remove the stitch from the left needle.

Increase: Yarn Over

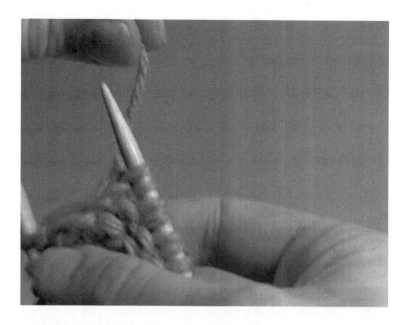

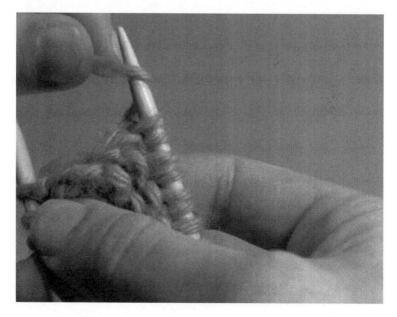

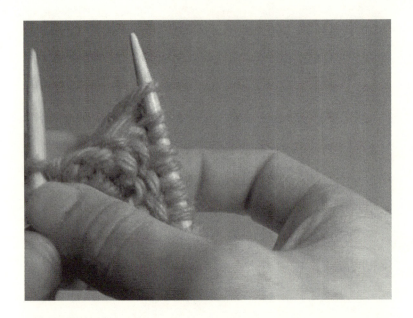

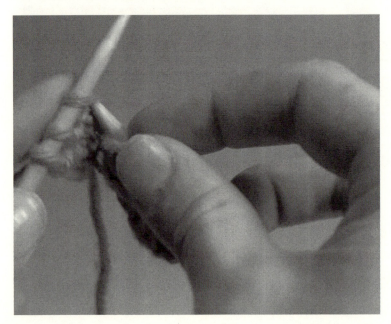

Yarn Over: this technique leaves holes in yarn. It is usually done for decorative stitches. When you want to leave an eyelet in your yarn use this technique.

- Knit a stitch

- Wrap yarn once around right needle to make an extra loop on right needle.

- Continue knitting.

Decrease Stitches

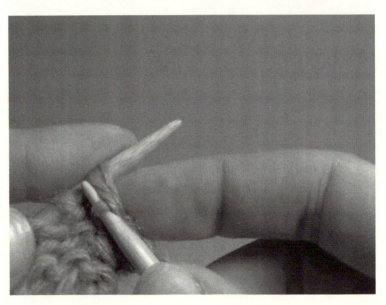

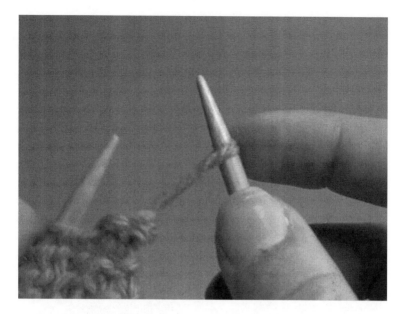

Knit Two Together: everything is the same as making a knit stitch, but instead of passing the needle through the top stitch on the left needle, pass the needle through the top two stitches and knit as if it were one stitch.

Decrease KRPR

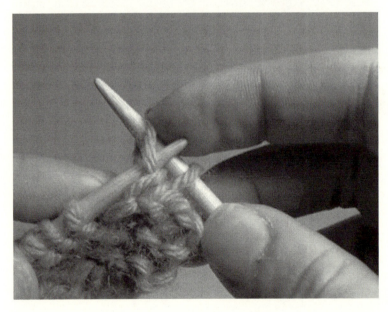

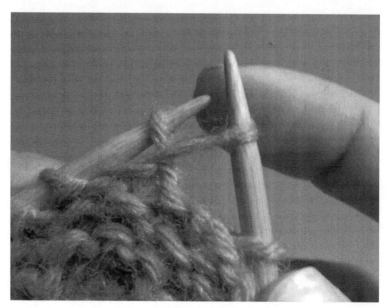

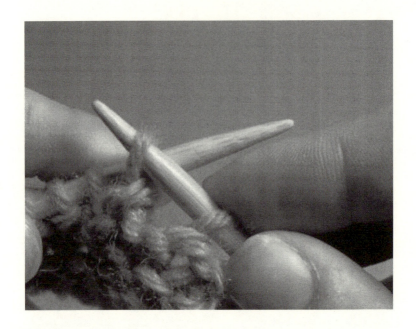

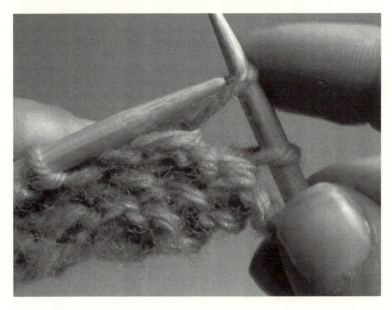

KRPR= Knit, Return Pass, Return

- *Knit* one stitch

- *Return* stitch you just knitted back on to the left needle

- Take the second stitch on left needle using your right needle and **pass** it over the top stitch on the left needle and off the needle.

- *Return* top stitch on left needle back to right needle.

3. Changing Color

Many patterns ask for a change in color of the yarn – or you may choose to do it yourself to add a unique quality to your projects. A guide for how to do this is presented below.

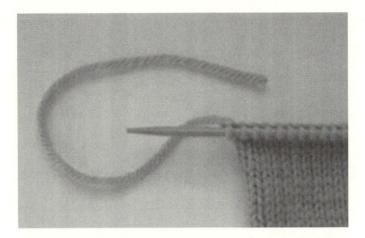

At the end of the row, cut the yarn leaving a tail about 20cm long.

At the beginning of the next row, slip the tip of the right needle into the first stitch on the left needle in the usual way. Loop the new yarn around the tip of the right needle.

Work the first three or four stitches on the row using the new yarn, keeping hold of the tails at the end of the row as you knit so that your stitches do not unravel. After knitting the few stitches, tie the tail ends in a knot to secure at the end of the row.

Now continue knitting the row as normal with your new color.

4. Sewing in Loose Ends

Sewing in the loose ends of your knitting can be done in many ways – eventually you will find your own preferred method. Here is a step-by-step guide to a few of these to get you started.

A one color garment presents no problem as to where to sew in the yarn. Unless you have some join in the fabric of the knitting, all the threads will be on an edge, and edges are where the seams or bands occur. These ends are easily sewn into the seams.

You can also make the ends vanish by using a sharp pointed needle with a large eye. Undo any loose knots you might have made when adding in a new end. Usually, there are two ends at one point. With one end, push the threaded needle through the edge of the rows that make the ridge of the seam. Pull the thread through and cut it off closely. Repeat with the second end in the opposite direction along the seam. Basically, you are burying the ends in the seam.

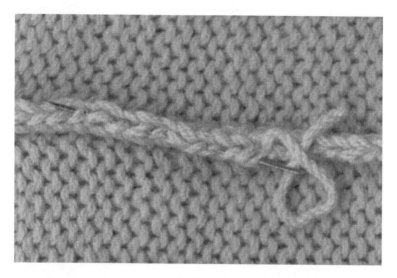

Sometimes you have a short end that will be impossible to thread into the needle and then sew in to the seam. Push the unthreaded needle along the seam starting from where the end is sticking out, then thread the end into the eye and pull the end through.

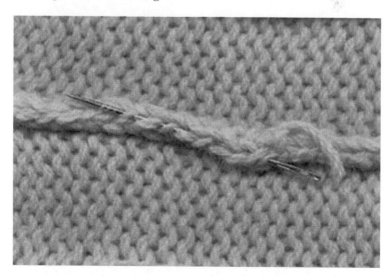

Seams should be as fine as possible so that they will have the same flexibility as the knitted fabric. For this reason, it is important to make sure that the ends don't add too much thickness to the seam. The ends will stay perfectly in place as long as you make sure that you have buried them adequately in the seam. Also, take the ends some distance along the seam. If they are too short, they could work their way out more easily. Don't weave an end around the edge stitches of the seam, it will always unweave with wear.

Don't sew any ends over and over the seam. This will only make a big lump that could stick out under the seam on the right side, and won't hold any better than using a sharp needle and sewing the thread firmly through the ridge of the seam.

If you have used two or more colors, sew the ends in to the matching col-ored seam. If you have sewn in the ends properly, you shouldn't even glimpse a sewn-in end on the right side, but this is extra insurance.

Color changes, patches or a knitted-in design result in ends located in the fabric of the garment. These should also be sewn in to the matching color on the wrong side, but now you don't have a seam to hide the ends.

Make a tiny stitch on the back at the base of the end, then carefully push the needle through matching stitches along the horizontal color change row, or vertically along the side of the color patch.

Matching the color will mean there is less of a chance that the ends will show through on the right side.

5. Dropped Stitches

It is inevitable that you will accidently drop a stitch at some point, so it's useful to know how to rectify this mistake. It doesn't matter where about you do it, there is a fix as shown below.

Down a Row – Knitwise

Insert your left needle through the front of the dropped stitch so it won't travel any farther.

Insert the left needle under the loose strand directly above the dropped stitch.

With the right needle, pull the dropped stitch over the strand and tip of the needle.

Now knit the stitch on the left needle.

Down a Row – Purlwise

Insert the left needle into the purl st.

Insert the left needle under the loose strand. It should now be to the right of the dropped stitch on the left needle.

With the right needle, lift the dropped stitch over the strand and the point of the needle.

Pull the strand through the stitch.

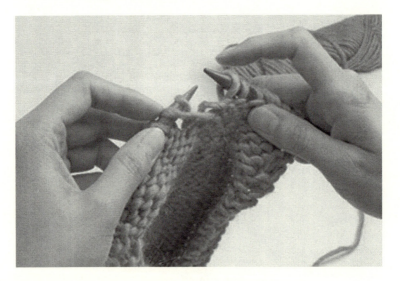

Transfer the stitch back to the left needle and purl it.

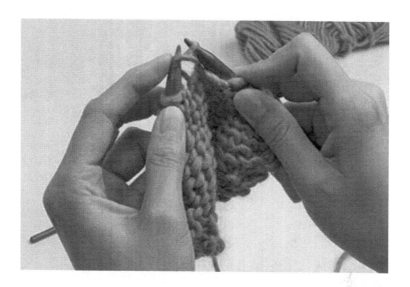

Several Rows Down

Position your work so you're above and at the same vertical point as the dropped stitch on the knit side of your work. Pull the needles apart very gently, exposing the horizontal lines from each of the rows missing the stitch.

Look at your work carefully, and assess how many rows the stitch has fallen. The sample shows 4 loose strands, representing 4 rows.

With the crochet hook inserted into the dropped stitch, hook the strand right above the stitch and pull it through.

Pull next strand through, and repeat until all the stitches are picked up from the previous rows.

Repeat this process until you're at the same row as the needles. Place the last stitch on the left needle, and continue in the stitch pattern.

Sometimes a knitting mistake is too big and you need to unravel what you've done to fix it. Below is a brilliant method for doing this:

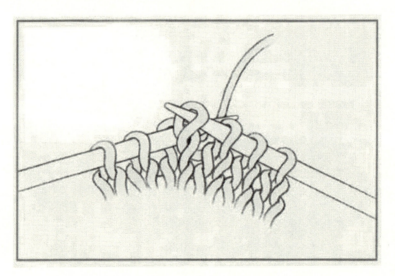

On a knit stitch, holding the yarn in the back, insert the left needle into the stitch one row below the first stitch on the right needle. On a purl stitch (not shown), hold the yarn in front and insert the needle from the back of the work. Slip the stitch onto your left needle, gently pulling the yarn out of the stitch above it. Continue in this way until you have reached your mistake.

6. Knitting in the Round

Knitting in the round is **often required for patterns**. You can do it on circular needles or double pointed needles. Once you have mastered this technique, a lot more pattern opportunities will open up to you. Garment patterns often need you to know a little about this.

Below are the best ways to do this:

Circular Needles:

To knit in the round using a circular needle, cast on the number of stitches you need and keep them close to the tip of the needle on the left side. Place a stitch marker on the right side of the needle.

Make sure not to twist your stitches. If you knit the cast on while twisted you create a mobius shape versus a tube. Next, hold the right side needle and join the round by knitting into each stitch. Move the stitch marker as you reach a new round.

When you are knitting in the round, you are always working on the "right side" of the fabric. Flat knit patterns may need to be altered to achieve the same results. If the pattern calls to purl the "wrong side," you would knit these instead. To knit in stockinette on circular needles, you are knitting every round.

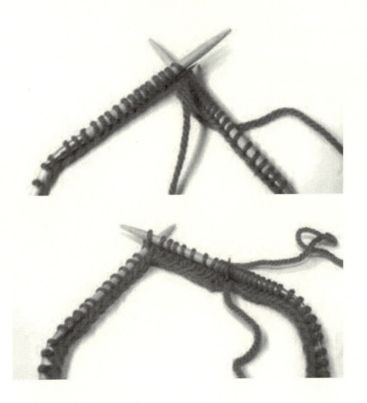

Double Pointed Needles:

To begin knitting in the round with double pointed needles, cast on the number of stitches you need onto one needle. Slip one third of the stitches purlwise onto a second double pointed needle. Repeat with the third double pointed needle, leaving the stitches divided across the three needles.

Join the stitches, being careful not to twist them. Make sure the cast on edge is pointing down on all needles. Push the stitches on the left hand needle down to the tip closest to you. These are the stitches you will be knitting first.

Insert the fourth needle into the first stitch on the left hand needle. Knit one and place a marker to note the beginning of the round. Now you have joined in the round on double pointed needles. Continue to knit across each of the needles, moving the marker as you reach a new round.

Some people prefer to knit with four needles, three with the stitches on and a fourth to work the stitches and some prefer five needles, four with a fifth to work the stitches. Sometimes your project will dictate how many needles you will need to use.

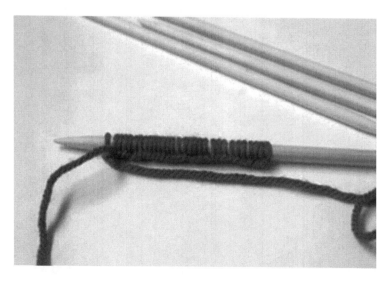

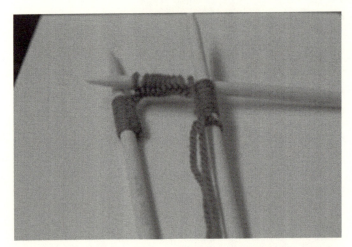

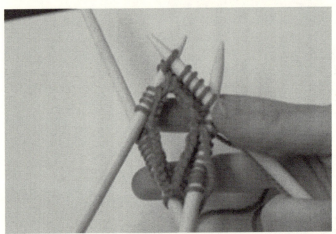

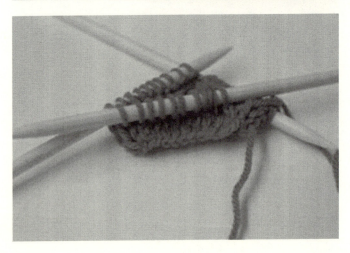

Magic Loop Method:

This technique was developed by Sarah Hauschka and Bev Galeskas. It allows you to create a small tube on one circular needle by using the more of the needle and less of the cable.

First you need a 32" cable needle. Next, cast on the number of stitches needed and slide them down onto the cable. Bend the cable so the stitches are divided in half and slide them back onto the needles. You should have roughly an even number of stitches on each needle.

With the needle tips pointing right and parallel, your yarn will hang in the back of the stitches. Pull on the needle that is holding the back stitches and draw up enough slack on the cable to allow you to use that needle tip to work the stitches on the front needle.

Knit all of the stitches on the front needle, being careful that you haven't twisted the stitches around on either needle. (The cast on edge should be visible all around the bottom.) Continue around. Each time the working yarn ends up to the right of your stitches, it is a new round.

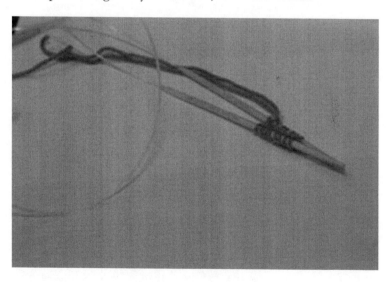

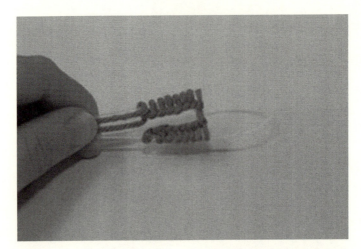

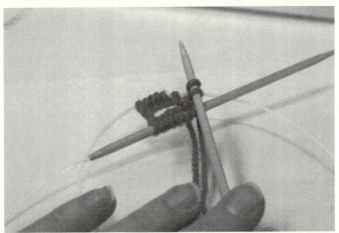

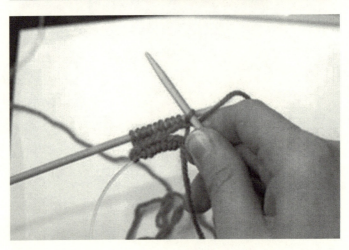

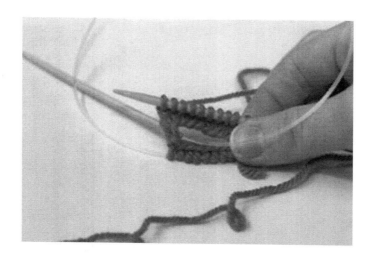

7. Sewing Knit Pieces Together

There will be times where you will need to sew some knitted pieces together. There are preferred ways to do this which produce a smoother result, as shown below.

Garter Stitch

To join two pieces together, thread a darning needle with the same yarn used to make the garment. Place the edges of the garment side by side with the right sides (the sides that people will see) facing out.

Stitch up the sides as shown, alternating from side to side.

Stockinette Stitch

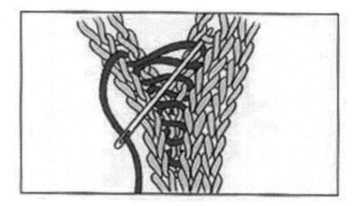

With the right sides (knit sides) facing you, begin seaming as for the beginning illustration of joining garter stitch. Working from side to side, go under the horizontal bar one stitch in from the edge as shown.

Shoulder Seams

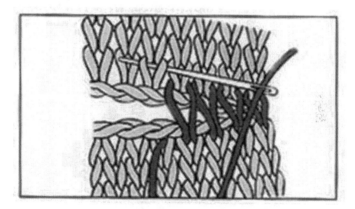

With the right sides facing you, align the shoulders and insert the yarn needle under one complete stitch as shown. Work inside the bind-off edge for a seamless look.

8. Sewing on Buttons

When creating knitwear, such as cardigans, you will want to attach buttons. The best way to do this so that the garment maintains its professional appearance is shown below:

First, gather these items: a needle that fits into the hole of your button, thread in your desired color and a pair of scissors.

Begin by placing your button to correspond with the buttonhole. Thread your needle.

Step 1: Insert the needle, from back to front, up through one hole. Leave a small tail on the wrong side of your sweater.

Step 2: Push the needle through the other hole of the button, down through the knitting to the back of the sweater. Pull tight.

Repeat these two steps 2 to 3 more times.

Step 3: Flip your sweater over so you can work on the back. You'll notice a tight loop has resulted from Steps 1 and 2.

Step 4: Insert your needle through the loop we saw in Step 3. From below, insert it through and out the other side. Repeat this step twice more.

Step 5: This is my own little extra step. Cut your thread so that it is the same length as the tail. Place both tails into the eye of your needle together. Weave those two ends through one or two stitches of your knitting, just to secure them.

Step 6: Snip the tails a centimeter or two away from the knitting – that will allow the ends to "settle" into the knit.

9. Making Pom Poms

Pom poms are really easy to create and are a brilliant edition to hats, bags and other accessories.

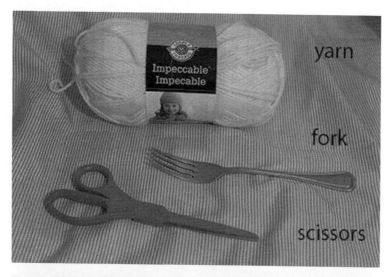

All you need to make a pom pom is yarn, a fork, and some scissors. If you want to make larger pom poms, you'll need a bigger fork, like a salad serving fork.

To start with, wrap the yarn around the fork as many times as you'd like.
The more you do it, the bigger your pom poms will be.

For small pom poms, wrap the yarn around the fork about twenty times. Keep your wraps tight. Also, be sure to center your wraps in the middle of the fork, leaving space at the bottom and top of the fork. If you want a fuller pom pom, or you're creating a larger pom pom, wrap the yarn around more (the large pom poms pictured previously were wrapped around a larger spoon 50 times).

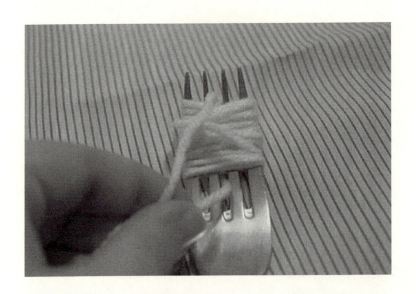

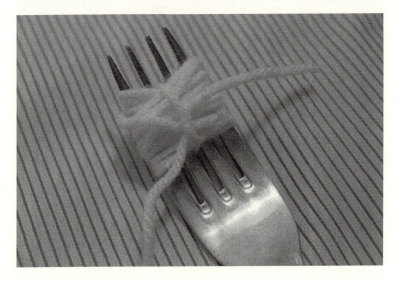

Cut the yarn and hold the wrap in place. Take another piece of yarn that's a couple of inches long and thread it through the bottom of the fork from front to back. Then pull it underneath the wrap and back over the top until the ends of the yarn meet. Now tie them together.

Pull the wrap off of the fork pull the knot tighter. The wrap will begin to curl and turn flat and round. The yarn will also make a bunch of tiny loops. Tie another knot on top of the other one just to secure things up.

Now, take your scissors and put them under the little loops created in the rounded ball of yarn. As you cut the loops, you'll see the pom pom begin to form.

Once you've cut all of the loops, go around the pom pom and cut any pieces of yarn that may be sticking out too far. Make sure the pom pom symmetrical.

10. Multicolor

There are many reasons that you wish to knit with more than one color; the pattern calls for it or maybe you just want to create something unique. There is a technique for this, known as '***stranding***', which is where you knot with 2 or more strands of yarn at once. This can also be done to thicken the same color yarn. The best methods to do this are shown below.

Two Balls of Yarn

The **most obvious way** of working with two yarns at once is to simply hold two strands of yarn together from two separate balls of yarn.

Advantages

If you **purchase your yarn already in balls**, you don't have to do much just find the ends and go!

If you want to do some interesting yarn combinations (such as hold **one strand of plain yarn together with one strand of beaded yarn-** which I've done when knitting a felted bag), no additional work needs to be done.

Since the balls of yarn are independent, it's okay if one ball is longer/shorter than another. Just work on a new second ball when one runs out.

You can hand-wind your balls of yarn. Since you can work from the outside of the yarn, there's no need to make center-pull balls (which either require a ball winder or a specialized hand-winding technique).

Disadvantages

Balls can sometimes be unruly. With this technique, some people struggle with keeping both balls of yarn in the same place, or keeping them from becoming hopelessly tangled. If you want to avoid this, consider winding two center-pull balls, and only working from the center. This eliminates (at least lessens the amount of) the 'rolling-around factor'.

If you purchase your yarns in skeins, you'll need to wind two skeins at a time to work in this technique. This **can sometimes be inconvenient.**

If you're working on a small project that doesn't need two balls worth of yarn, this technique requires modification. You can divide your yarn in half, and work with two smaller balls, but in my opinion, this eliminates the 'easy advantage' of this technique.

Work from Two Ends of a Center-Pull Ball

A **second technique** is to work from both ends of a center-pull ball: holding the yarn that comes from the center together with the yarn that comes from the outside.

Advantages

You only need to wind one ball of yarn at a time: particularly great if your project requires only one ball of yarn, or an odd number of balls.

You can do this 'straight off the shelf' with many yarns packaged as balls-most are center-pull.

Disadvantages

You'll need to make center-pull balls… which either require a ball winder or a specialized hand-winding technique.

This, like working with two balls at once, can sometimes become tangled and a little unruly.

Winding Two Balls Together

A third technique is to wind two balls of yarn together, and then knit or crochet with the two ends.

Advantages

This technique is easy to work from: no ends or stray balls to get tangled.

You can hand-wind your balls of yarn. Since you can work from the outside of the yarn, there's no need to make center-pull balls (which either require a ball winder or a specialized hand-winding technique).

If you purchase your yarn in skeins, winding two yarns together takes half the amount of time as winding two separate balls of yarn.

Disadvantages

If you purchase your yarn already in balls, this technique takes extra time to get started.

If you're working on a small project that doesn't need two balls worth of yarn, this technique requires modification. You can divide your yarn in half, and then wind these two smaller balls together…but that makes this technique more time-intensive.

11. Tension

Controlling the tension in your yarn whilst knitting is a really useful skill to master as it will make everything else come much easier and many more of your projects will be successful. Practicing with the knitting gauge is the best way to do this.

First, try a few different needles of different material to get the gauge and tension that is best for your project. If your stitches are sliding off the needle willy-nilly, you might need to go down a size or two. If your stitches just won't budge, try a smoother material like aluminum.

Keep a loose grip on the yarn as you knit. Don't tug on the yarn as you complete each stitch. If you'd like your fabric to be more dense, go down a needle size or two rather than trying to knit tighter.

Maintain even tension by consciously focusing on your knitting rhythm for the first few minutes after you pick up your needles. Knitters who like to watch movies or listen as they knit find their tension getting too tight during a chase scene or too loose during a song and dance number. Commuter knitters find their tension changes from the ride to work and their ride home. Unless you like your knitting to be a diary of your day, pay attention to the way you begin to knit; that will keep your hands focused even while your eyes wander.

12. Blocking

Blocking in knitting is the process of using water or steam to shape your project to its final size and shape. Check the yarn label – if it says '*dry clean only*' you cannot use blocking.

Hand Blocking

Stretch the knitting horizontally, vertically, and diagonally, several times in each direction. You will be able to see progress after a few rounds; the stitches should appear more evenly spaced. Different fibers call for different amounts of elbow grease, so don't yank on lacey cashmere as you would ropey linen! The key is to simply watch the knitting and adjust your strength accordingly.

Pin and Spray

Lay your knitting out on the towel. If it is a shaped piece, a sweater back, for example, you may want to stretch it slightly into the shape you desire. If it is a scarf or other simple rectangle, lay it down so that it is flat, but not stretching unnaturally.

Begin to pin around the edges of your knitting, being careful to maintain the shape you want. Once you have pinned around all sides, spray the piece with water and leave it to dry. Be patient! It may take a few hours, or even overnight.

Heavy Duty Blocking

If you have a hat that's a hair too small, or a sweater a few rows too short, you may want to try a more aggressive blocking technique.

Rather than pinning and spraying the piece, submerge it in a bath of room temperature water.

Remove to a clean towel and roll it to get out excess water. Don't wring or twist the knitting while it is weak and wet! Be gentle!

Hand block the damp knitting to the desired size and pin it into place. Let it dry thoroughly.

KNITTING PATTERNS

This chapter will give you a selection of knitting patterns to practice. They are ranged from beginner to more advanced, but you'll be able finish them all in approximately 3 days using the stitches you have previously completed in this book.

1. Cowl Scarf

Difficulty: Beginner – pattern is reversible.

Size: 19 inches circumference, 11 inches tall.

Yarn: 2 balls of wool yarn, size 4.

Needles: Size 13.

Tools Required: Yarn, needle.

Gauge Instructions: 16 stitches = 4 inches

Pattern: Knit with both balls of yarn together – the stranding method.

Cast on 43 stitches.

On the right side of the **first row**:

- Knit 2 stitches

- Purl 1

- Knit the rest of the row until 4 stitches away from the end.

- Purl 1

- Knit 2

On the wrong side of the **second row**:

- Slip 1 stitch

- Then, with the yarn in the front, purl 1

- Knit 1

- Purl 1 then double stitch – repeat 9 times

- Purl 1

- Knit 1

- Purl 2

On the right side of **row 3**:

- Slip 1 stitch

- With the yarn in the back, knit 1

- Purl 1

- Knit the rest of the row until 4 stitches away from the end.

- Purl 1

- Knit 2

Row 4:

- Slip 1 stitch

- With the yarn in the front, purl 1

- Knit 1

- Purl 2

- Purl 1, then double stitch – repeat this 8 times

- Purl 3

- Knit 1

- Purl 2

Row 5: Repeat the instructions for Row 3.

Repeat all these row instructions listed above 16 times.

Cast off.

2. Knitted Beanie

Difficulty: Beginner

Size: Adult sized.

Yarn: 100 yards of medium worsted weight, size 4.

Needles: Size 8.

Tools Required: Yarn, needle.

Gauge Instructions: 16 stitches = 4 inches.

Pattern:

- Cast on 74 stitches

- For the first 6 rows create a rib stitch across – knit 1, purl 1

- Then knit one row and purl the next until the piece measures 7 inches, from the cast on edge. Be sure to purl the last row

- For the next row, knit 2 together (k2tog) across

- Purl the next row

- K2tog across for the next row

- Cut 12 inches of yarn and thread it onto the yarn needle

- Carefully pull the last row of knitting from the needle and thread the needle though every stitch, Pull tightly then stitch the seam shut.

3. Baby Blanket

Difficulty: Beginner – pattern is reversible.

Size: 30 inches wide, 33 inches long.

Yarn: 5 balls of chunky yarn – size 5.

Needles: A circular needle, size 10.

Tools Required: Stitch markers, a large eye blunt needle.

Gauge Instructions: 12 stitches and 20 rows = 4 inches

Pattern: NB – the circular needle is used to accommodate the large number of stitches so **work back and forth as if working on straight needles.**

Cast on 90 stitches

For the **first 6 rows**, knit the seed stitch:

- For the first row, knit one and purl one all the way across

- For the second row, purl the knit stitches and knit the purl stitches and repeat this 4 times

Row 7 – work the seed stitch over the first 5 stitches for the side border

Purl 16 stitches

Knit 16; purl 16 all the way across until the last 5 stitches

Work the seed stitch for the final 5 stitches

Row 8 – work in the seed stitch in the first and last 5 stitches, and knit across in between

Rows 9 to 160 – repeat rows 7 and 8

Row 161 to 166 – repeat instructions for the top 6 rows, making the seed stitch for the top border

Bind off and weave in the ends.

4. Fingerless Mittens

Difficulty: Beginner – pattern is reversible.

Size: 10 inches around and 18 inches long.

Yarn: 2 balls of worsted weight yarn.

Needles: Size 7.

Tools Required: Yarn, needle, stitch markers.

Gauge Instructions: 20 stitches and 28 rows = 4 inches.

Pattern:

Cast on 66 stitches

For the **first row**:

- On the right side knit 2 stitches

Then purl 2 and knit 2 all the way across

For the **second row**:

- Purl 2

- Purl 2 and knit 2 all the way across

For the **third row**, which is a *decreasing row*:

- Knit 1

- Slip 1 stitch

- Knit across until the last three stitches

- Knit 2 together

- Knit 1 (up to 48 stitches as rows progress)

For the **fourth row**, which is an *increasing row*:

- Knit 2 stitches

- Make 1 stitch, then knit 2 and make another stitch

- Knit 20 stitches (up to 44 stitches as rows progress)

- Repeat these rows until the piece measures 14 inches.

- Then, you need to create the thumb opening:

- Knit 20

- Bind off 12 stitches

- Knit 20

For the **next row**:

- Purl 20

- Cast on 2 stitches

- Purl 20 stitches

- Repeat this for 2 more inches, then bind off before sewing the piece together.

Repeat all of this once more for the second glove.

5. Dishcloth

Difficulty: Beginner – pattern is reversible.

Size: Approximately 10x10 inches.

Yarn: 2 balls of worsted weight yarn in different colors.

Needles: Size 8.

Tools Required: Yarn, needle.

Gauge Instructions: 12 stitches and 20 rows = 4 inches.

Pattern: Your 2 colors will be described as 'color A' and 'color B'.

With your color A, cast on 34 stitches

Knit 3 rows

For the **first row**, on the right side:

- With color B, knit 3 stitches

- Knit 2 and slip 2 stitches – with the yarn in the front, repeat until final 3 stitches

- Knit 3

For the **second row**:

- With color B, knit 3 stitches

- Slip 2 stitches, then with the yarn in the front purl 2 stitches – repeat until final 3 stitches

- Knit 3

Knit **the third and fourth rows** across with color A

For the **fifth row**:

- With color B, knit 3 stitches

- Slip 2 stitches, then with the yarn in the back knit 2 – repeat until the final 3 stitches

- Knit 3

For the **sixth row**:

- With color B, knit 3 stitches

- Purl 2 stitches, slip 2 – then, with the yarn in the front repeat until the final 3 stitches

For the **seventh and eighth rows**, knit across with color A

Repeat rows 1 – 8 until the piece is approximately 8 to 10 inches

With color A, knit 3 rows

Bind off.

6. Baby Bib

Difficulty: Beginner – pattern is reversible.

Size: Approximately 6x8 inches.

Yarn: 1 50g ball of worsted weight yarn.

Needles: Size 7.

Tools Required: Yarn needle, crochet hook.

Gauge Instructions: 16 stitches = 4 inches.

Pattern:

Cast on 30 stitches

Knit across **rows 1, 3 and 5**

For **rows 2, 4 and 6**:

- Increase the first stitch

- Knit across to the last stitch

- Increase the last stitch

For **rows 7, 9 and 11**:

- Knit 4 stitches then purl 4 stitches – repeat until the last 4 stitches

- Knit 4 stitches

Rows 8, 10 and 12:

- Knit 4 stitches

- Knit 4 stitches

- Purl 4 and knit 4 alternatively across until the last 4 stitches

- Knit 4 stitches

Rows 13, 15 and 17:

- Knit 4 stitches

- Knit 4 stitches

- Purl 4 and knit 4 alternatively across until the last 4 stitches

- Knit 4 stitches

Rows 14, 16 and 18:

- Knit 4 stitches

- Purl 4 stitches

- Knit 4 and purl 4 alternatively across until the last 4 stitches

- Knit 4 stitches

Repeat rows 7 to 18 two more times

Repeat rows 7 to 12 once

The next row:

- Knit 14 stitches

- Cast of 8 stitches

- Knit 14 stitches

For the shoulders (do this twice):

For **the first row:**

- Knit 2 together

- Knit 10 stitches

- Knit 2 together

Knit across all the even numbered rows

Row 3:

- Knit 2 together

- Knit 8 stitches

- Knit 2 together

Row 5:

- Knit 2 together

- Knit 6 stitches

- Knit 2 together

Row 7:

- Knit 2 together

- Knit 10 stitches

- Knit 2 together

Row 9:

- Knit 2 together

- Knit 2 stitches

- Knit 2 together

Row 11:

Knit 2 together

Crochet a single chain tie.

7. Headband

Difficulty: Beginner – pattern is reversible.

Size: Adult sized 21 inches to 22 inches.

Yarn: One ball of super bulky, size 6 yarn.

Needles: Size 15.

Tools Required: Yarn, needle.

Gauge Instructions: 11 stitches = 4 inches

Pattern Notes:

For the front cable or fc:

- Slip 3 stitches to cable needle and hold in the front

- Knit 3

- Knit 3 from cable needle

- For the back cable or bc:

- Slip 3 stitches to cable needle and hold in the back

- Knit 3

- Knit 3 from cable needle

Pattern:

Cast on 15 stitches loosely

For the **first row**, on the wrong side:

- Knit 1

- Purl 13

- Knit 1

For the **second row**:

- Knit 1

- Slip 1 stitch with the yarn in the back, then knit 1 – repeat this 7 times

Repeat rows 1 and 2 until the piece measures roughly 6.5 inches

Cable row 1 and all odd numbered rows on the wrong side:

- Knit 1, purl 6, knit 1, purl 6, knit 1

Cable row 2:

- Knit 1

- Back cable

- Purl 1

- Front cable

- Knit 1

Cable rows 4 and 6:

- Knit 7

- Purl 1

- Knit 7

Knit rows 1 to 6 three times

Knit rows 1 to 3 once more

Row 1, on the right side:

- Knit 1

- Slip 1 stitch with the yarn in the back, then knit 1 – repeat 7 times

Row 2:

- Knit 1

- Purl 13

- Knit 1

Knit these final 2 rows until the piece measures approximately 6.5 inches.

Bind off loosely

Block, seam and tuck in any ends

8. Hand Puppets

Difficulty: Intermediate.

Size: Small.

Yarn: A small amount of size 2 yarn in a color of your choice. Plus some of the following colors for the add-ons; orange, green, red and a contrast color for the rabbits features.

Needles: Size 0.

Tools Required: Yarn, needle.

Gauge Instructions: 18 stitches = 2 inches.

Pattern:

Cast on 24 stitches over 3 double pointed needles

Join, being careful not to twist

Purl 2 rows

Knit across the next row until the finger puppet is the size you desire (adult size – 3 inches)

Top decreases:

- Knit 2 stitches together across the row (12 stitches remain)

- Knit 2 stitches together across the row (6 stitches remain)

- Cut the yarn leaving a 10 inch tail

- Thread the yarn needle and draw through the remaining stitches

- Weave in the ends

Then, make 2 bunny ears in either the main color or pink:

- Cast on 10 stitches

- Bind off

- Attach to top of rabbit puppet and shape how you like

For the carrots:

- Do a 4 stitch l-cord for 5 rows

- Decrease by knitting 2 stitches together twice across the row to 2 stitch l-cords for 2 rows

- Cut yarn and attach to rabbit puppet

- Add some green stitching for carrot tops

For the tail:

On the back of the puppet, create a pom pom and attach

For the rest:

- Use French knots for the eyes and nose and attach with the needle

- Split plies of yarn for the whiskers

To add the heart, use the following knitting chart:

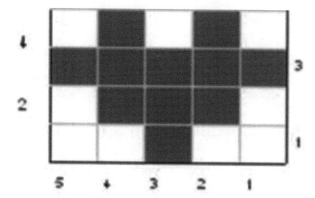

9. Baby Booties

Difficulty: Intermediate.

Size: Approximately 6 – 12 months old.

Yarn: 1 ball of size 3 yarn.

Needles: Size 7.

Tools Required: Yarn, needle.

Gauge Instructions: 9 stitches and 25 rows = 4 inches.

Pattern:

Cast on 2 stitches

For the **first row** – and **all alternate rows** – knit across on the wrong side

For the **second row:**

- Knit 1

- Bring the yarn forward making 1 extra stitch

- Knit 12 stitches

- Bring the yarn forward making 1 extra stitch

- Knit 1

- Bring the yarn forward making 1 extra stitch

- Knit 12 stitches

- Bring the yarn forward making 1 extra stitch

- Knit 1

For the **fourth row**:

- Knit 1

- Bring the yarn forward making 1 extra stitch

- Knit 14 stitches

- Bring the yarn forward making 1 extra stitch

- Knit 1

- Bring the yarn forward making 1 extra stitch

- Knit 14 stitches

- Bring the yarn forward making 1 extra stitch

- Knit 1

For the **sixth row**:

- Knit 1

- Bring the yarn forward making 1 extra stitch

- Knit 16 stitches

- Bring the yarn forward making 1 extra stitch

- Knit 1

- Bring the yarn forward making 1 extra stitch

- Knit 16 stitches

- Bring the yarn forward making 1 extra stitch

- Knit 1

Knit 11 rows of the garter stitch

For the toe:

Row 1:

- Knit 15 stitches

- Knit 2 together

- Knit 5

- Slip 1 stitch

- Knit 1

- Pass slipped stitch over

- Slip 1 stitch

- Bring the yarn to the front of the work

- Turn the work

Row 2:

- Knit 2 together

- Knit 5

- Slip 1 stitch

- Knit 1

- Pass slipped stitch over

- Bring the yarn to the front of the work

- Slip 1 stitch purlwise

- Turn the work

Row 3.

- Knit 2 together

- Knit 5

- Slip 1 stitch

- Knit 1

- Pass slipped stitch over

- Slip 1

- Bring the yarn to the front of the work

- Turn work

The fourth row is the same as row 2

Row 5.

- Knit 2 together

- Knit 5

- Slip 1 stitch

- Knit 1

- Pass slipped stitch over

- Slip 1 stitch

- Turn the work

Row 6.

- Purl 2 stitches together through back loops

- Purl 5

- Purl 2 together

- Slip 1 stitch purlwise

- Turn the work

Repeat rows 5 and 6 for the **seventh and eighth rows**

Row 9.

- Knit 2 together

- Knit 5

- Slip 1 stitch

- Knit 1

- Pass slipped stitch over

- Knit to the end of the row

Purl across the **tenth row**

Continue in the garter stitch for 2 inches, ending with a wrong side row

Cast off

Sew the sole seam to finish off

10. Leg Warmers

Difficulty: Intermediate – pattern is reversible.

Size: Adult sized.

Yarn: 1 ball of worsted weight yarn.

Needles: Size 8 circular needles.

Tools Required: Yarn, needle.

Gauge Instructions: 5 stitches = 1 inch.

Pattern:

Cast on 48 stitches and join to work in the rounds

Work in 2x2 rib stitching for 4 inches

Knit the next round

Round 1:

- Knit 6 stitches

- Knit 2 together

- Yarn over

- Repeat all above until the end of the round

Round 3:

- Knit 5 stitches

- Knit 2 together

- Yarn over

- Knit 1

- Repeat all above until the end of the round

Round 5:

- Knit 4 stitches

- Knit 2 together

- Yarn over

- Knit 2

- Repeat all above until the end of the round

Round 7:

- Knit 3 stitches

- Knit 2 together

- Yarn over

- Knit 3

- Repeat all above until the end of the round

Round 9:

- Knit 2 stitches

- Knit 2 together

- Yarn over

- Knit 4

- Repeat all above until the end of the round

Round 11:

- Knit1 stitches

- Knit 2 together

- Yarn over

- Knit 5

- Repeat all above until the end of the round

Round 13:

- Knit 2 together

- Yarn over

- Knit 6

- Repeat all above until the end of the round

Cast off

Repeat all for the second leg warmer

11. Cushion Cover

Difficulty: Intermediate – pattern is reversible.

Size: 17x17 inches.

Yarn: 8 balls of size 3 yarn to be held double throughout.

Needles: Size 11.

Tools Required: Yarn, needle, buttons, crochet hook.

Gauge Instructions: 11 stitches = 4inches

Pattern:

Hold the yarn double and cast on 45 stitches

Row 1:

- Knit 2

- Purl 1, knit 1 all the way across until the last stitch

- Knit 1

Purl the **second row** across

Row 3:

- Knit 1

- Purl 1, knit 1 right across

Purl the **fourth row** across

Repeat these 4 rows until the piece measures 39 inches

Bind off loosely

Fold up the bottom, leaving 4 inches at the top

Sew together the sides

If you wish to add buttons, do so, the weave in ends

12. Children's Socks

Difficulty: Intermediate.

Size: Hell to toe is 6.5 inches.

Yarn: 2 balls of size 4 yarn in 2 colors.

Needles: Size 2 double pointed needles.

Tools Required: Yarn, needle.

Gauge Instructions: 32 stitches and 42 rows = 4 inches.

Pattern:

For the cuff:

- Cast on 48 stitches

- Distribute these over the needles and join in the round

The leg of the sock is worked in the rib stitch – knit 1, purl 3, use this for the following rounds:

- 10 rounds in the main color

- 6 rounds in the 2nd (contrasting) color

- 6 rounds in the main color

- 4 rounds in the 2nd color

- 6 rounds in the main color

- 2 rounds in the 2nd color

- 8 rounds in the main color

For the heel flap, purl 1 stitch onto the previous needle

Then for the **first row**:

- Slip 1 stitch

- Knit 22 stitches

Turn your work (put the remaining 25 stitches onto spare 2 needles or a stitch holder)

For the **second row**:

- Slip 1 stitch

- Purl 22

- Repeat these 2 rows eight more time

For the **turn heel**:

Row 1:

- Slip 1 stitch

- Knit 14

- Slip slip knit

- Knit 1

- Turn the work

Row 2.

- Slip 1 stitch

- Purl 7

- Purl 2 together

- Purl 1

- Turn

Row 3.

- Slip 1 stitch

- Knit 8

- Slip slip knit

- Knit 1

- Turn

Row 4.

- Slip 1 stitch

- Purl 9

- Purl 2 together

- Purl 1

- Turn

Row 5:

- Slip 1 stitch
- Knit 10
- Slip slip knit
- Knit 1
- Turn

Row 6:

- Slip 1 stitch
- Purl 11
- Purl 2 together
- Purl 1
- Turn

Row 7:

- Slip 1 stitch
- Knit 12
- Slip slip knit
- Turn

Row 8:

- Purl 13 stitches
- Purl 2 together
- Purl 1

For the *instep*:

- Knit 15 stitches of the heel

- Knit 13 stitches down the edge of the heel

- Work 25 stitches of the pattern

- Pick up and knit 13 stitches up the other side of the heel

- Knit 7 and place a marker

- Rearrange the stitches so that there are 21 on the 1st needle, 25 pattern stitches on the 2nd needle and 20 stitches on the 3rd.

Knit 6 rounds, continuing the rib pattern on needle 2

Using needle 1:

- Knit to the last 3 stitches

- Knit 2 together

- Knit 1

Using needle 2, work the rib pattern

With needle 3:

- Knit 1

- Slip slip knit

- Knit to the end of the round

Knit with needles 1 and 3

Knit the rib pattern with needle 2

Repeat all of this 5 more times

Continue without decreasing until the foot measures approximately 1½ inches

For the toe, use the 2nd color

End off the rib pattern on needle 2

For the first round, knit on all needles

For the second round:

Using needle 1:

- Knit until the last 3 stitches

- Knit 2 together

- Knit

Using needle 2:

- Knit 1

- Slip slip knit

- Knit to the last 3 stitches

- Knit 2 together

- Knit 1

Using needle 3:

- Knit 1

- Slip slip knit

- Knit to the end

Repeat these 2 rounds five more times

Repeat round 2 four more times

Bind off and sew in any ends

13. Sweater

Difficulty: Intermediate.

Size: 6 – 9 months.

Yarn: 100g of worsted weight yarn.

Needles: Size 8 double pointed and circular needles.

Tools Required: Yarn, needle, stitch markers, stitch holder, a button.

Gauge Instructions: 22 stitches = 4 inches.

Pattern:

For the body:

Cast on 34 stitches using the circular needle

Row 1:

- Knit front and back

- Place marker

- Knit front and back

- Knit 4 stitches

- Knit front and back

- Place marker

- Knit front and back

- Knit 18

- Knit front and back

- Place marker

- Knit front and back

- Knit 4

- Knit front and back

- Place marker

- Knit front and back

Purl across the **second row**

Row 3:

- Knit 1

- Yarn over

- Knit front and back

- Slip marker

- Knit front and back

- Knit 6

- Knit front and back

- Slip marker

- Knit front and back

- Knit 20

- Knit front and back

- Slip marker

- Knit front and back

- Knit 6

- Knit front and back

- Slip marker

- Knit front and back

- Yarn over

- Knit 1

Purl the **fourth row** across

Row 5:

- Knit 1

- Yarn over

- Knit to stitch before the next marker

- Knit front and back

- Slip marker

- Knit front and back

- Knit to stitch before the next marker

- Knit front and back

- Slip marker

- Knit front and back

- Knit to stitch before the next marker

- Knit front and back

- Slip marker

- Knit front and back

- Knit to stitch before the next marker

- Knit front and back

- Slip marker

- Knit front and back

- Knit to last stitch

- Yarn over

- Knit 1

Purl the **sixth row** across

Repeat rows 5 and 6 until there are 50 stitches between the 2d and 3rd markers across the back

For the sleeves:

- Knit 1

- Yarn over

- Knit to the first marker

- Place the sleeve stitches onto the waste yarn

- Place marker

- Knit back stitches

- Place the other sleeve stitches onto the waste yarn

- Place marker

- Knit to the last stitch

- Yarn over

- Knit 1

Purl the next row across

For the lower body:

Row 1:

- Knit 1

- Yarn over

- Knit to the last stitch

- Yarn over

- Knit 1

Purl the second row across

Repeat rows 1 and 2 until there are 50 stitches on both front panels (the sections outside of the markers) 15 0 stitches in total

Knit across the next row

For the side tie:

Row 1:

- Knit to the first marker

- Slip marker

- Knit front and back

- Slip first stitch on right needle back to the left

- Place the next stitch on the right needle on a stitch holder placing the holder to the right side of the work

- Slip the first stitch back onto the right needle

- Knit to end

Row 2:

- Knit to stitch before the second marker

- Knit front and back

- Slip first stitch on the right needle back to the left

- Place the next stitch on the right needle on a stitch holder, placing the holder to the right side of the work

- Slip the first stitch back onto the right needle

- Slip marker

- Knit to end

Row 3:

- Knit to first marker

- Slip marker

- Knit front and back

- Slip first stitch on right needle back to the left

- Place the next stitch on the right needle on a stitch holder, placing the holder on the right side of the work

- Slip the first stitch back onto the right needle

- Knit to the end

Knit the **fourth row** across

Bind off loosely

For the sleeves:

- Evenly space the sleeve stitches on 3 double pointed needles

- With the right side facing, locate the centre bottom of the sleeve opening

- Pick up 2 stitches from the left of the opening and continue knitting the round, picking up 2 additional stitches onto the needle – 40 stitches in total

- Knit 2 more rounds

Then you need a decrease round:

- Knit 1

- Knit 2 together

- Knit to last 3 stitches

- Slip slip knit

- Knit 1

Decrease every fourth round a further 8 times

Knit 4 more rounds

Purl 1 round, knit 1 round for the next 4 rounds

Bind off loosely

For the side tie:

- Join yarn to 3 stitches on the stitch holder

- Knit inches of garter stitch

- For the next row, knit 2 together then knit 1

- For the last row, knit 2 together then thread the yarn through the remaining stitch

For the front tie:

- Pick up 3 stitches from the edge of the garter stitch section of the right front section

- Repeat

Finishing:

Weave in ends

Sew the button on the inside of the right hand flap.

14. Bag

Difficulty: Advanced.

Size: Approximately 8x18 inches.

Yarn: 1 ball of worsted weight yarn.

Needles: Size 4 double pointed.

Tools Required: Yarn, needle, buttons (if required).

Gauge Instructions: 12 stitches and 20 rows = 4 inches.

Pattern:

For the body:

- Cast on 72 stitches

- Bring the first stitch and the last stitch together

- Place a marker between these 2 stitches

- Join together and start knitting in the round by knitting the first stitch right after the last stitch

- Knit in the round until the piece measures 17cm. The body of the bag is basically a square. If the width of the bag is more than 17cm, then knit till the height is the same as the width.

For the Handles:

- Adjust the first 18 stitches onto a single needle

- Then, knit these 18 stitches as follows: K2, P2, K10, P2, K2

- Turn and knit the same 18 stitches as follows: P1, K1, P1, K1, P10, K1, P1, K1, P1

- Repeat these 2 rows until the handle measures 25cm

- Using kitchener stitch, graft these 18 stitches to 18 stitches next to it.

- Once grafted, cut off the yarn and weave the ends into the bag neatly

- Start step 2 and 3 again with the next 18 stitches

- Repeat these 2 rows until the handle measures 13cm

- Using kitchener stitch, graft these 18 stitches to the remaining 18 stitches on your circular needles.

Sewing up the bottom:

- Position the bag so that the shorter handle is in front of the longer one

- Sew up the bottom using mattress stitch

Attaching the buttons:

- Using a sewing needle, attach assortment of buttons to the body of the bag.

Lining the bag: Line the bag and it lasts longer. I lined both the handles and the body.

- Find any fabric that you can re-cycle. You can buy new fabric too but I think an old T-shirt works just fine. Measure and cut the fabric with about 1 inch extra for folding in. Two narrow strips for the handles and a long rectangle for the body.

- Position and pin the narrow strips to the inside of the handles right side facing up. Fold the 1-inch border in and slip stitch along all the sides.

- Fold the fabric for the body in half right-side together. Mark out the 1 inch border and stitch up the side and bottom. You can use the sewing machine for this if you have one. Turn it out so that the right side is facing out. Turn the knot bag wrong side out and slip the body lining in. Fold the 1-inch border and pin along the opening of the bag over the handle lining.

Remember, sew the buttons or any other ornaments that you like onto the bag first before you line it because you want to hide all the threads and endings underneath the lining.

15. Tank Top

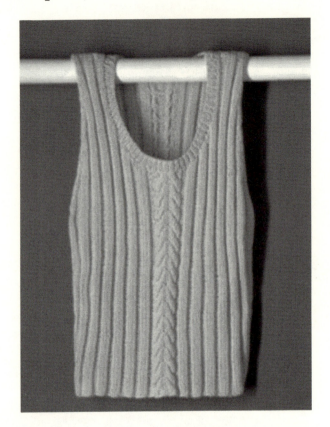

Difficulty: Advanced – pattern is reversible.

Size: Adult sized – approximately 32 inches across.

Yarn: 2 balls of size 5.

Needles: Size 8.

Tools Required: Stitch holder, cable needle.

Gauge Instructions: 22 stitches and 30 rows = 4 inches.

Pattern: *As this is the advanced section, the patterns will be written as they normally are

BACK

Using 3.25 mm needles cast on 86[92 : 98 : 104] sts and work in patt as follows:

1st Row: P1[0 : 1 : 0], K3[1 : 3 : 1], (P3, K3) 6[7 : 7 : 8] times, P1, K4, P1, (K3, P3) 6[7 : 7 : 8] times, K3[1 : 3 : 1], P1[0 : 1 : 0].

2nd Row: K1[0 : 1 : 0], P3[1 : 3 : 1], (K3, P3) 6[7 : 7 : 8] times, K1, P4, K1, (P3, K3) 6[7 : 7 : 8] times, P3[1 : 3 : 1], K1[0 : 1 : 0].

3rd Row: As 1st row.

4th Row: As 2nd row.

Change to 4 mm needles and proceed in patt for remainder of Back as follows:

1st Row: P1[0 : 1 : 0], K3[1 : 3 : 1], (P3, K3) 5[6 : 6 : 7] times, P3, C6F, C6B, P3, (K3, P3) 5[6 : 6 : 7] times, K3[1 : 3 : 1], P1[0 : 1 : 0].

2nd Row: K1[0 : 1 : 0], P3[1 : 3 : 1], (K3, P3) 5[6 : 6 : 7] times, K3, P12, K3, (P3, K3) 5[6 : 6 : 7] times, P3[1 : 3 : 1], K1[0 : 1 : 0].

3rd Row: P1[0 : 1 : 0], K3[1 : 3 : 1], (P3, K3) 5[6 : 6 : 7] times, P3, K12, P3, (K3, P3) 5[6 : 6 : 7] times, K3[1 : 3 : 1], P1[0 : 1 : 0].

4th Row: As 2nd row.

5th Row: As 3rd row.

6th Row: As 2nd row.

These last 6 rows form patt for remainder of Back.

Keeping patt correct and working inc sts in rib for 1st and 3rd Sizes and in stst for 2nd and 4th Sizes inc 1 st at each end of 3rd row and every foll 12th row until 96[102 : 108 : 114] sts are on needle.

Work 11 rows straight in patt. Place a marker at each end of last row to mark beg of armholes.

SHAPE ARMHOLES

1st Row: K2, skpo, patt to last 4 sts, K2tog, K2.

2nd Row: P3, patt to last 3 sts, P3.

3rd Row: K3, patt to last 3 sts, K3.

4th Row: P3, patt to last 3 sts, P3. **

Rep last 4 rows (inclusive) until 72[76 : 80 : 84] sts rem ending with 4th row then 1st and 2nd rows 1[1 : 1 : 0] time more. = 70[74 : 78 : 84] sts.

SHAPE NECK

Next Row: K3, patt 17[18 : 20], turn.

Complete first side as follows:

*** Cont to dec 1 st at armhole edge as before on 2nd row, **at the same time** dec 1 st at neck edge on next 5 rows. = 14[15 : 17] sts.

Cast off.

Sl center 30[32 : 32] sts onto a st holder.

With RS facing rejoin yarn at neck edge of rem 20[21 : 23] sts and patt to last 3 sts, K3.

Complete second side to correspond with first side from ***.

FRONT

Work exactly as given for Back to **.

Rep last 4 rows (inclusive) until 86[92 : 96 : 102] sts rem, ending with 4th row.

SHAPE NECK

Next Row: K2, skpo, patt 29[31 : 33 : 35], turn.

Complete first side as follows:

***** Keeping patt correct cont to dec 1 st at armhole edge as before on every 4th row, **at the same time** dec 1 st at neck edge on next 6 rows and foll 4 alt rows.= 19[21 : 23 : 25] sts.

Keeping neck edge straight cont to dec 1 st at armhole edge as before on every 4th row (from previous dec) until 14[15 : 17 : 18] sts rem.

Work 3[3 : 3 : 1] rows straight in patt.

Cast off.

Sl center 20[22 : 22 : 24] sts onto a st holder.

With RS facing rejoin yarn at neck edge of rem 33[35 : 37 : 39] sts and patt to last 4 sts, K2tog, K2.

Complete second side to correspond with first side from *****.

NECKBAND

With a backstitch join right shoulder seam.

Using 3.25 mm needles and with RS facing rejoin yarn and pick up and K32[35 : 35 : 36] sts evenly from left side of front neck (approx 4 sts from every 5 rows along straight edge and 1 st from every st/row along shaped edge). Work across sts from front neck st holder as follows: K6[7 : 7 : 8], K2tog, K4, skpo, K6[7 : 7 : 8]. Pick up and K32[35 : 35 : 36] sts evenly from right side of front neck and 6 sts from right side of back neck.

Work across sts from back neck st holder as follows: K11[12 : 12 : 13], K2tog, K4, skpo, K11[12 : 12 : 13]. Pick up and K7 sts evenly from left side of back neck. = 123[133 : 133 : 139] sts.

1st Row: P1, *K1, P1, rep from * to end.

2nd Row: K1, * P1, K1, rep from * to end.

1st and 2nd rows form rib.

Work 2 rows more in rib.

Cast off fairly loosely in rib (WS).

TO MAKE UP

See ball band for pressing and washing instructions.

With a backstitch join left shoulder seam and neckband seam.

With a backstitch join side seams to markers.

Allow the 3 sts of stst at armhole edges to roll onto wrong side to form rolled edges around armholes.

TOP 5 TIPS
FOR BEGINNERS

So now that you have experimented with a few knitting patterns, you may have stumbled across a few issues. With that in mind, this chapter covers a few tips to help you avoid, or at least overcome them.

1. Start Big

Starting with chunky yarn and big needles because then it will be easy to spot mistakes and unravel what you've done.

2. Invest in Equipment

Don't go nuts getting absolutely everything available because you will end up buying a lot of equipment you don't need. But, be sure to get:

- 2 pairs of needles

- Stitch markers

- A selection of basic, inexpensive yarn

- A sewing needle

- A bag or box to keep everything in

3. Online

There are many resources online which can help you get started. This book gives you all of the basics but there will come a point where you want more. Aside from YouTube which is filled with extremely useful videos from fellow knitters, the following websites are filled with useful information and other patterns to practice:

www.knittinghelp.com

www.knittingpatterncentral.com

www.lionbrand.com

4. Find a Friend

Having someone to knit with is always helpful. You can make the activity more sociable. If you don't know anyone who knits, there is a huge online community where people swap tips and discuss projects. A few of these forums include:

www.knittingforums.org.uk

www.knittinghelp.com/forum

www.ravelry.com

5. Abbreviations

Keep a list of all the knitting abbreviations listed in this book handy for completing patterns. It's easy to forget what some of them might mean. If patterns include unusual or pattern specific abbreviations, they will list them.

LEFT-HANDED
KNITTING

Don't be put off from knitting just because you are left-handed. It is very easily modified, as shown by this guide:

Instead of casting on to the left-hand needle, you cast on to the right-hand.

The needle you work with is the left-hand needle while the right-hand needle holds the stitches you're working into. **Knitting** and **purling** are the same concepts, where you still either work with the yarn behind your needle or in front of it. Your right side and wrong side of the fabric are still the same based on where those yarn bumps belong. A left-handed knitter just has to figure out how to make all of these basics feel natural without as much guidance as a right-handed knitter would find. Many left-handed knitters find that working in a mirror is great practice and helps them figure out the best ways to work.

THE 3 MOST COMMON KNITTING MISTAKES

Now we're going to look at some of the **most common mistakes in knitting and how to fix them.**

1. *Stitches are Too Tight*

One very common complaint that new knitters have is that their stitches are just getting too tight. There are a *few ways to overcome this:*

- Make sure you aren't knitting at the tips of your needles.

- Be sure to push the needle through the stitch correctly.

- Adjust the tension.

2. *Fixing Incorrect Stitches*

To fix a knit stitch make sure that the stitch from the previous round is on the left and the loose strand is on the right.

Then insert the right needle tip into the stitch from front to back, and pull the stitch over the loose strand and off the needle. The stitch is now complete.

To fix an incomplete purl stitch make sure that the stitch from the previous round is on the right and the loose strand is on the left. Insert the right needle tip through the stitch from back to front and slip the stitch to the right needle. Tip the right needle down slightly in front of the loose strand.

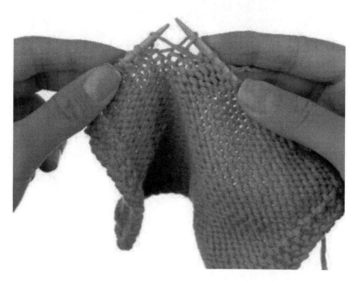

Push the loose strand through the stitch from front to back.

Place the stitch back onto the left needle and now it is ready for you to work.

Did you accidentally knit a stitch instead of purl it, or vice versa? Did you also not realize your mistake until you're on the next round? Fixing this mistake is a variation on picking up a dropped stitch.

Take the incorrect stitch off the left needle. Gently pull the strand of yarn running between the two needles. This pulls the stitch out by 1 round.

Pick up the stitch correctly. For a knit stitch, insert a crochet hook or the tip of a knitting needle into the stitch from front to back and pull the strand back through the loop to re-form the stitch.

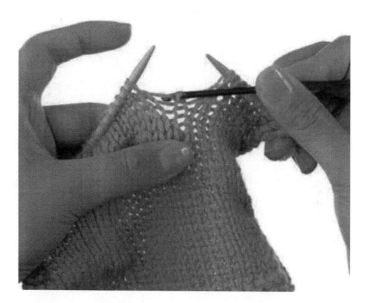

For a purl stitch, place the loose strand in front of the stitch. Insert a crochet hook or tip of a knitting needle into the stitch from back to front.

Pull the strand through the loop from front to back. Place the corrected stitch back onto the left needle.

When working with some yarns, you can easily pick up only part of the yarn strand while knitting along. To correct a split stitch on the next round, take the stitch off the left needle and then replace it, taking care to place the needle through the entire stitch. To correct a split stitch several rounds down, ladder down and pick up the stitch in pattern, taking care to pull the entire strand through on each round when working back up to the needle.

3. Twisted Stitches

If your knitting stitches end up twisted, you will want to be able to fix them.

In a non-twisted stitch, the part of the stitch in front of the left needle appears to the right of the part of the stitch behind the needle. Sometimes, especially when picking up dropped stitches, the stitch ends up with the front leg to the left of the back leg, which creates a twisted stitch.

You can correct a twisted stitch in two ways.

Take the stitch off the left needle, turn it, and place it back onto the needle; it is now untwisted.

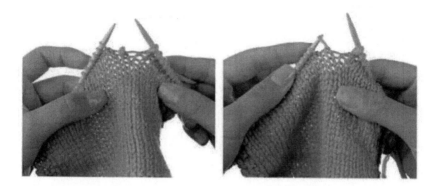

You can also correct a twisted knit stitch by knitting into the back of the stitch rather than the front. Insert the right needle tip into the stitch on the left needle through the back loop from right to left; the right needle is behind the left needle.

Wrap the yarn as for a knit stitch and pull the new stitch through from back to front. The stitch is now untwisted and correctly mounted for the next round.

When working in the round on double-points, two circular, or one long circular, sometimes *"gaps"* or *"ladders"* form at the junction of two needles. Pulling the needles in opposite directions creates tension on the stitches, which causes a gap.

The laddering effect is often more pronounced when using double-pointed needles because there are more junctions — four rather than the two you get when working with circulars.

To prevent ladders, pull the working yarn firmly on the first 2 stitches when switching needles. This helps to tighten the corners.

If you are still having trouble, try shifting the stitches from needle to needle as you knit around. This prevents a ladder effect because you disperse the loose stitches over the entire sock. However, some patterns assume that the stitches on each needle remain on the same needle for the course of the sock. Just make sure your stitches are on the right needles when knitting a heel or toe.

Knit to the last 2 stitches of the needle (double-pointed or circular).

Slip the last 2 stitches onto the next needle, taking care not to twist them, then knit across the next needle as usual to the last 2 stitches.

Repeat Step 2 as you go around to shift the stitches from needle to needle.

SOURCES

www.loveknitting.com

www.deramores.com

www.knitpicks.com

Yarn Forward
Encouraging Your Creativity

www.yarnfwd.com

Knitting-Warehouse
The Discount Yarn & Notions Warehouse

www.knitting-warehouse.com

www.woolwarehouse.co.uk

sewing-online.com

sewing-online.com

Laughing Hens

www.laughinghens.com

www.knitandsew.co.uk

FAQ

1. Why is knitting a good skill to have?

Knitting is a brilliantly useful skill that can help you create a wide variety of your own products – everything from toys to clothing. But, not only that, it's scientifically proven to improve your mood, mind and body. It's a therapeutic skill which you will not regret learning!

2. How do you read a knitting chart?

The best way to read a knitting chart is discussed in detail in this guide, in the <u>Knitting Charts</u> chapter.

3. What I need to buy to start off knitting?

The <u>Supplies</u> chapter of this guide gives you the basics of what you need to start knitting. However, the yarns, needles and anything extra you'll need for a specific pattern will be listed as one of the first pieces of information.

4. How do you do double-pointed knitting?

Double pointed needles are generally used for knitting in the round on projects that are too small for circular needles. They are often purchased in sets of 5. Here is a brilliant guide for how to use them, with these main top tips:

- Cast on to 1 double pointed needle.

- Then slip ½ the stitches onto another needle.

- Then a third onto another.

- Use a fourth needle to knit.

5. Does it cost a lot to knit?

Knitting can be done very cheaply **if you know the right places to look**. Local haberdashery stores will sell a wide range of products from high quality to budget so it really is a skill that applies to everyone.

6. What is an easy way to learn how to knit?

The step-by-step guides provided in the <u>Stitches</u> chapter of this guide will get you started. If you need extra help, check out some of the online <u>Sources</u> provided.

7. What is the Garter stitch in knitting?

A brilliant guide to completing the Garter Stitch can be found in this guide at <u>Garter Stitch</u> chapter.

8. How do you knit with 3 needles?

You will often use 3 or more needles when working with double pointed needles. The topic has been discussed in this guide.

9. What are the differences for English and continental methods for knitting?

Everyone has their own preference when it comes to knitting style. You will eventually develop your own.

English Knitting

- Hold yarn in right hand

- Throw yarn when wrapping

- Easier with chunky weight yarns

Continental Knitting

- Hold yarn in left hand

- Pick the yarn when wrapping

- Faster when you're knitting the knit stitch

- Alternating stitches is easier

- Easier for crocheters to learn

10. Where can I find stretch knit fabric?

Your local haberdashery store will sell all sorts of fabrics, including stretch knit. There will also be many online resources, such as <u>moodfab-rics.com/fashion-fabrics.</u>

11. What is knitting in tandem?

Tandem knitting is a technique for knitting socks or gloves or anything in the round that comes in pairs and uses 9 DPNs, it casts on for both items in the pair at the same time, and involves completing a portion of one of the pair, then the same portion of the other item of the pair.

12. Is it hard to knit a scarf?

In the <u>Patterns</u> chapter of this guide, you will find a pattern for a knitted scarf designed specifically for beginners. Scarves can be made by anyone at any skill level. If you're an advanced knitter, your creations can be much more complex and embellished.

13. Is crocheting harder than knitting?

Crocheting **is a different skill to knitting** in the way that it uses one hook rather than two needles. Different people prefer different skills so practicing both is the best way to figure out which one you personally find easier and more suitable.

14. Where can I find some great knitting patterns?

Knitting patterns can be found in haberdashery stores, but they are also available in abundance online. Just type '*Knitting Patterns*' into any search engine and you will be spoilt for choice.

15. What are the next steps once you've worked through this guide?

This book gives you all the basics you need for starting knitting. Once you have gotten to grips with all of the stitches and patterns provided, it is time to move on to more complex patterns – you can maybe even create your own! Once you have mastered this skill, the possibilities are endless.

CONCLUSION

This guide has now given you a **solid basis of knitting to work from**. It has provided you with step-by-step guides for basic and advanced stitches, special techniques and even a wide range of patterns. Once you have worked through these, you will have a much better understanding of knitting and how it can benefit you and your life. Now you can **create your very own garments, home wares and even toys** which give you the opportunity to make some very special gifts for yourself and your friends and family.

Hopefully you have discovered some interesting knitting techniques that you want to try and some cool patterns to experiment with. Once you master all of the basic stitches and manage to put them together in a cohesive successful manner, **you will be able to progress on to just about everything**. Enjoy!

ABOUT THE AUTHOR

Knitting has always been considered an old woman's game. But that was not the case with Emma Brown. As soon as she could hold a needle, her mother was trying to teach her how to knit. Though it took her a couple of years, until she could really maneuver those needles, once she had it down, she was a knitting machine.

Throughout her childhood, she was sitting beside her mother, and they would knit, day in and day out. For Christmas, all of her brothers and sisters received handmade socks and her friends all received colorful hats. For the first few years, they were lumpy and a little messy, but by age ten, she was a wizard with the yarn and the needles.

In her teenage years, Emma discovered that many of her friends wanted to learn to knit. She gathered them up around her kitchen table, with needles in hand, and tried to teach them how to knit, just as her mother had taught her, all those years ago. They had all arrived with a different project in mind, and they all looked to her for guidance. As they stumbled over their first stitches, it was then when she first realized that there must be a better way. With everyone struggling to make a different project, she knew it would be nearly impossible to teach them all effectively.

That is when she first came up with the idea to find a better way to teach knitting. She had been told by several people that knitting seemed so difficult, that it was something you could learn if you had hours and hours a week to spend learning it. But she knew that it couldn't actually be that difficult. Millions of people already knew how to do it—it couldn't be that hard to teach!

Instead of again trying to teach her friends the way her mother had taught her, she began devising a new method. As she knitted, she realized that socks were the perfect tool for teaching knitting. They included all of the basic techniques, and what you learned from sock knitting, you could easily use to follow just about any knitting pattern. She began writing down everything that could be learned from her knitting, and then gathered her friends together again. With needles in hand, she explained the basic steps, and within three days, every last one of her friends had a brand new pair of socks, knitted by hand.

Now, you can tap into the same knowledge, draw on Emma's years of knitting experience, and learn the most amazing knitting patterns in a quick and easy way!